M000033198

PROPHECY SPEAKS

Dissolving Doubts

EARLE ALBERT ROWELL

REVIEW AND HERALD® PUBLISHING ASSOCIATION
Since 1861 | www.reviewandherald.com

CONTENTS

FOREWORD

Earle Albert Rowell, to whom we are indebted for this story of David Dare and his experiences in Bible research, is also author of *The Bible in the Critics' Den, Letters From a Converted Infidel to His Agnostic Father,* and *Battling the Wolves of Society.* He was reared in an infidel home, and was himself a converted infidel. For a number of years he lectured on the Pacific Coast, following the plan of going into a city, advertising his meeting, inviting all classes of unbelievers to attend, and to interrupt him with questions at any time during the lecture. These he promised to answer. The story of David Dare is a composite of these experiences, and is based on actual facts.

—The Publishers

Bible texts credited to Moffatt are from: *The Bible: A New Translation,* by James Moffatt. Copyright by James Moffatt 1954. Used by permission of Harper & Row, Publishers, Incorporated.

CHAPTER 1

THE SCOFFER SCOFFS

George Emerson turned to his father and pointed an emphatic finger at an advertisement he had just read. Amazement was in his voice: "Read that, Dad."

The elder Emerson took the paper and read aloud, his tone growing more amusedly cynical as he followed the item:

"INFIDELITY CHALLENGED AND REFUTED.

"An unusual lecture by David Dare, a converted infidel. All skeptics, scoffers, unbelievers, infidels—all classes of doubters—are especially invited to hear this important address. They may interrupt the speaker at any time during his lecture with questions or with denials of his statements. If you are a freethinker, agnostic, heretic, or atheist, COME! THIS MEETING IS ESPECIALLY FOR YOU."

The father laid the paper down, contempt in his manner. "This fellow certainly takes in a lot of territory."

"Well, he includes you, Dad! Here is your opportunity," said George gleefully. "You are always asking Christians, and particularly ministers, all kinds of hard questions that they can't answer. Let's go and hear this man. I have some questions I'd like to ask him too." George's questions, however, were hazy, and born of the desire to see his father in action.

"It isn't likely he'd welcome my questions, George," smiled the father confidently, with slight emphasis on "my."

"But the invitation is 'especially' to skeptics, who are urged to come with their questions," argued the son eagerly.

"Yes, I know—a very fine gesture it is, too," admitted Henry Emerson.

"You don't believe he means it? You think it's a trick to get a crowd?"

"Something like that. I never heard of such a meeting. If he lives up to the terms of his advertisement, the meeting will run away with him."

"But let's go and see for ourselves," urged George. "You might be surprised."

"Of course we'll go," assented his father, "since you are so anxious. No doubt the place will be packed."

Mr. Emerson himself was in reality eager to attend, but hid his longing under an apparently reluctant consent to accompany his son.

George was a wide-awake, questioning youth of twenty who had been reared in an atmosphere of religious doubt. The elder Emerson was a large, rather dogmatic man of average education, with a keen mind turned slightly cynical.

While they were discussing the strange announcement, Mrs. Emerson and her daughter, Lucile, entered. Mrs. Emerson was a motherly woman of the home-keeping type. Lucile was a pert lass of eighteen, thoroughly "modern" and sophisticated beyond her years, who amazed her father, horrified her mother, and delighted her brother.

"Another religious argument," she laughed, her quick eye taking in the slightly belligerent attitude of her father.

"Wrong guess, sis," George assured her. "Just the prelude to one that promises to be a wholesale affair."

"A wholesale religious argument!" exclaimed Lucile in puzzled amazement. "What in the world do you mean?"

"Fellow here in the paper, a converted infidel, advertises to take on all comers—at the same time," explained George, with twinkling eyes.

"Explain yourself, sir," demanded his sister in some hauteur. "Talk sense!"

"Read this," he replied, thrusting the advertisement into her hands.

She read with increasing astonishment to the end. "H'mm! A large order. He can't do it! Must be a religious mountebank," she decided.

"No, for the meetings are sponsored by substantial, conservative citizens whose names are appended further on—see," said George, pointing them out.

Lucile cast a roguish eye at her father, but addressed her brother. "I see where Dad is going to be as happy as any well-trained iconoclast could possibly be."

"It's tonight; will you go?" George spoke eagerly, as he drew his sister to one side.

"Is Dad going?"

"Yes."

"Then try to keep me away. I see where Dad is riding for a fall!"

"You think so?" exclaimed George.

"Do I think so?" she mimicked. "I am sure of it. Do you think any man would dare to insert such an advertisement, sponsored by these people, unless he knew his—his—"

"Bible," George hastened to add, as they dashed off to get ready.

Though the Emerson family arrived fifteen minutes early, it was with difficulty that they found seats in the large auditorium.

"Standing room only, pretty soon," whispered George to Lucile.

"I am curious to see how they are going to conduct such a strange meeting as this," remarked Mr. Emerson, settling himself comfortably.

"We won't have long to wait—there they start for the platform now," indicated Lucile. "I'm just thrilling with excitement."

"Why," exclaimed Mr. Emerson in surprise, "Dr. Morely is chairman of the meeting. David Dare must have an important message to induce the city's most prominent physician to introduce him."

Just then Mr. Dare, a man past thirty and of above-average height, walked briskly, but with utter lack of self-consciousness, to his place beside Dr. Morely, who engaged him in conversation while the crowd continued to gather.

"Look!" cried Lucile as Dare turned his face in their direction. "Mr. Dare appears anything but contentious. Not the least as I expected. He seems as calm as if he were sitting by his own fireside with a friend."

"Did you expect him to look like a bloodthirsty gladiator or to give the outward evidence of an inward brainstorm?" chaffed her brother.

"Of course not," she flashed, "but is it possible he realizes there is a seething volcano of questions ready to erupt the moment he begins?"

"At any rate, he does not seem disturbed by the thought. I imagine he knows better than you what awaits him, and that his poise is the result of confidence born of experience."

The chairman called the meeting to order. "A series of lectures entitled 'Infidelity Challenged and Refuted' will be given here every Sunday afternoon for the next few weeks," began Dr. Morely crisply. "This above all others is an age of doubt. The speaker, Mr. Dare, was reared in an infidel home. He was once an ardent skeptic. He has invited all classes of doubters here, and freely offers them opportunity to question his statements, even to the extent of interrupting him to propound their questions or denials. This is a serious attempt to aid skeptics in their search for the truth about the Bible. Mr. Dare will now tell you what he proposes to do."

An electric hush of expectancy swept the large audience as David Dare walked in calm dignity to the front. He stood silent for a few moments, scanning the sea of faces with his candid eyes.

"You are all here under a misapprehension of what I plan to do," he began.

"I knew it, I knew it," muttered Mr. Emerson as low exclamations of amazement swept the audience.

"Ah-ha !" exclaimed Lucile in an undertone, while George sat speechless.

"I am not here to challenge anyone. I do not challenge infidelity or infidels," he went on calmly. The audience stirred restlessly.

"Nor do I expect to refute infidels or infidelity." Dare's clear voice took on firmer tones. It could be heard above the belligerent murmurings that arose everywhere.

"This is a huge joke," snorted the elder Emerson disgustedly.

"We are wasting our time here. Suppose we go." He half arose.

"Nevertheless, infidels and infidelity will be challenged. Infidelity and infidels will be refuted," David Dare promised in a clear, ringing voice.

Those who had arisen sat down abruptly. "This sounds interesting," said Emerson. "Guess I'll stay."

The large audience was silent again, leaning eagerly forward to miss nothing. David Dare smiled in understanding of their attitude, sensing fully the shocked amazement, the amused contempt, the jeering mockery changed now to interested expectancy. Stepping calmly to the very edge of the platform, he spoke quietly, but in an earnest, impressive manner:

"Yes, doubters will be challenged and skepticism refuted, but not by me. The scoffers of today, the unbelievers in this very audience, were challenged and refuted many hundreds of years ago by One infinitely wiser than I.

"It will be my part to set before you certain facts. You will be given an opportunity to admit them, or invited to deny them if you can. Since every opportunity is granted to question the statements made—since you are freely invited, even urged, to interrupt the speaker at any time with inquiries or denials—your silence will be taken as assent to his statements. Is that not fair?"

"Yes, yes. Go on," impatiently responded a number in the audience.

"Your questions and denials must necessarily be confined to the subjects under consideration. These lectures are built up in logical sequence, and if you will attend the entire series, many irrelevant questions that may be suggested will probably be taken up later.

"I shall assume that we are all doubters, myself included. But we are honest explorers, adventurers together, seeking to learn the truth about this strange, dominating, disturbing book that has been put into our hands—the Bible. I am merely your captain on this voyage of discovery.

"And mark this: I shall use no material we are not all agreed upon. We will advance together, or not at all. If a statement is not accepted by everybody, it will be discarded immediately. We will progress as a unit.

"And further, I warn you that I expect to proceed step by step from infidelity to Christianity. You are invited to find flaws in this process. I am as anxious to find them as you are. I am fully as anxious to get help from you as to aid you. This is far too serious a matter for me to dare risk remaining in error. I earnestly invite your united help. Look for flaws in my reasoning and fearlessly point them out. If you fail to find any, I assume that you will as fearlessly accept the inevitable conclusion." Mr. Dare paused a moment for the audience to grasp his plan.

"An amazingly daring undertaking," exclaimed one.

"Absurd, impossible," sneered another.

"Fair indeed, provided he lives up to his promise," remarked Mr. Emerson. His sentiment was evidently shared by the majority present. Few, however, were convinced that the man who stood before them really meant what he said.

"All right, we are with you so far. Let's go," shouted a stentorian voice from the rear.

David Dare picked up a small, flexible leather book and held it toward the audience in his right hand. "Here is a book called the Bible. Unique claims are made for it. Its warm friends go so far as to maintain that it is the Word of God. Indeed, millions have cheerfully suffered horrible deaths rather than deny this or disregard its teachings. And other millions stand ready this minute to follow their example.

"Now, all of us here are doubters; but a book for which millions died, and are still ready to die, certainly ought to be examined. We are willing to investigate. Is this book open to questioning? Does it invite scrutiny?

"How are we to test a book for which such high claims are made? Where can we best begin? What part is most vulnerable? Does it boast qualities that make it different from every other book in the world?

"Suppose we turn to the book itself and see. Here I read, 'Prove all things; hold fast that which is good [1 Thess. 5:21]. Does anyone here disagree with that?"

Mr. Dare paused for reply. There was none.

"Good; we are together so far. 'Come now, and let us reason together, saith the Lord' [Isa. 1:18]. Even the most skeptical mind will admit the fairness of this invitation. Note that the reasoning is together. But God gives His reasons first so that we may 'prove' them. Does anyone here find fault with that?"

Again Mr. Dare paused for reply, but no one ventured.

"How are we to assay this volume? Have its writers given us any means by which to verify its statements? Do they especially invite or urge us to try any particular part? Does any portion claim to be impregnable?

"Naturally, if there is any section for which special claims are made, we shall investigate them. We are not now concerned with the statement that it is all the Word of God. We must take some part that we can put into the crucible for the acid test.

"If we, as Peter claims he did, could witness Christ's great glory, actually hear the voice of God speaking to His Son Jesus, we would consider we had very convincing evidence. However, Peter, telling of this experience [2 Peter 1:16-21], adds that there is evidence far more certain than even the audible demonstration of the presence of God. 'We have also a more sure word of prophecy.' And he concludes by saying, 'Prophecy came not in old time by the will of man: but holy men of God spake as they were moved by the Holy Ghost.'"

Mr. Emerson rose quickly, towering to six feet of impressive stature. A number over the audience, evidently interested in Dare's talk, shouted, "Sit down, sit down; put him out."

But a rising chorus of voices shouted encouragement: "Go on, speak up, friend." They were evidently glad that a test of the speaker's invitation to interrupt him was to be made so soon.

David Dare stopped immediately and turned smiling to the conspicuous figure awaiting recognition. He raised his hand. An expectant silence followed.

"All I ask," he said calmly, "is that you give your name, and make your statement brief and to the point. This applies to all who may speak hereafter. Now I shall be glad to hear you, sir."

All eyes turned to Mr. Emerson. He seemed to feel his importance as champion of the skeptic's cause, and appeared to stretch up an inch taller. In his manner was a serious dignity.

Lucile leaned over and whispered to George: "Dad is run fling true to form." George smiled assent, and put his finger to his lips.

"My name is Emerson. My statement will be brief and on the subject. But I doubt if you will be glad to hear me. However, you invited it. I am amazed that a man of your intelligence attempts to palm off on this audience such antiquated and exploded stuff as prophecy. There is no real prophecy. The facts are always twisted to fit the prediction. And if there is real accord, it is purely accidental. Finally, prophecy was usually written after the event, and made to fit into it. Anyone can write that kind of prophecy.

"I could easily now write a prophecy of Lindbergh's flight across the Atlantic, date it A.D. 1000, and credit it to some famous scientist of that time. Then, fifteen hundred years from now, when that prediction, presumably written nine hundred years before the event it foretells, is found, a fine case for accurate prophecy could be made out for that scientist."

"That's right, that's right," commended several voices as Mr. Emerson sat down. "A real poser. Sounds unanswerable."

All eyes now turned back to David Dare, who stood tranquilly by the stand, ready to answer.

Chapter 2

Challenge to a Prophecy Contest

If David Dare sensed the antagonism of the audience, he gave no evidence of it. He spoke calmly, but with the emphasis of sincere conviction.

"Prophecy, you say, is either vague or tricky, or just a shrewd guess. I grant you it is sometimes hard to understand, and I remember when I found it distressingly vague.

"But why do you apply a method of investigation to the Bible you would be ashamed to use with any other book? When you open a geometry book for the first time and glance at the section on solids, in your perplexity and despair you might defend your lack of understanding by claiming geometry to be vague. Yet it is the most crystal clear of all sciences in the world."

Mr. Emerson arose again. Mr. Dare paused and motioned for him to speak.

"Do you mean to imply that prophecy is as rigidly demonstrable as geometry?" he asked incredulously.

"Yes, I mean just that."

"You are making things unnecessarily hard for yourself. No one would think of setting such a task for you." Mr. Emerson's tone hinted jubilation combined with sympathy.

"It is not a task, but a pleasure," responded the lecturer, smiling. "Let us return to geometry. If you start with the simple problems at the beginning, you will later understand perfectly what you now confidently proclaim to be obscure.

"So it is with prophecy. Some prophecies naturally precede others. There are some predictions in the book of Revelation that it would be impossible to understand without a knowledge of Daniel.

"If prophecy is so easy to disprove, how is it that among all the thousands of books written by infidels there is not one in all the world devoted to showing specifically how Bible prophecies have failed? If these predictions are so easily proved to be the result of a clever or lucky guess, or if the fulfillment is merely the twisting of facts to fit the prediction, or if the prophecy were written after the events took place, and made to fit into them, how is it that facile skeptics, who are so alert for arguments against the Bible, have universally overlooked the one demonstrative method of proving the Bible to be false?

"Why has not some Tom Paine, some Robert Ingersoll, or some Mr. Emerson, for that matter, shown how utterly absurd, false, and contrary to fact are the prophecies of Moses concerning the Jews, of Isaiah about Babylon, of Ezekiel telling of the fate of Tyre and Sidon, of Jeremiah concerning Egypt and Palestine, of Daniel, with his amazing predictions about Rome and the nations into which Rome was to be divided, of Jesus concerning the growth of His kingdom and the spread of this very Bible unto every nation, kindred, tongue, and people?"

Mr. Emerson shot up eagerly. David Dare smiled his welcome. Lucile turned twinkling eyes to her brother.

"Anyway, the man's a good sport," she whispered.

"He seems to welcome these interruptions," admitted George.

"No one has replied to Bible predictions," said Emerson, in a strong, clear voice, "for the same reason that no one has replied to the Delphic oracle prognostications—not worth the trouble. Herodotus relates the story of Croesus consulting the famous Delphic oracle as to whether he should fight the Persians. He was told that 'by crossing Halys, Crocesus will destroy a mighty power.' He did: his own! And when Pyrrhus sought advice on a similar errand of war, he received this cryptic reply: 'I declare thee, O Pyrrhus, the Roman to be able to conquer.' Thus, no matter which way the battle went, the augury would be true. All prophecy everywhere is like that—amusing, sometimes ingenious, but never worth serious attention. But you make great claims for it."

"Bible prophecies are worthy of consideration because they are as far from Delphic utterances as midday from midnight," replied Mr. Dare. "Bible predictions burn all bridges. If the thing does not happen, no apology can be offered.

"Every other part of the Bible has been criticized in elaborate detail by unbelievers. But when it comes to prophecy, skeptics the world over content themselves with a wholesale, jaunty, contemptuous denial, as though it were of no consequence."

"Will you Christians risk anything on prophecy? What of consequence is at stake to believers?" asked Mr. Emerson.

"Just this: The Bible bases its whole claim to credence on the accuracy of its forecasts. Why have unbelievers never made a detailed study of them so that they might expose the fraud of prophetic chicane to the deserved contempt of the public, if the prophecies are what you claim?

"You, Mr. Emerson, along with other skeptics, despise prophecy. There were many such unbelievers in Paul's day. To them and to you he said: 'Despise not prophesyings. Prove all things; hold fast that which is good' [1 Thess. 5:20, 21]. Here you are challenged above all things else to prove prophecy—that is, test it, and if it prove true, hold fast to. it.

"But wherein are prophecies better evidence than miracles?" asked Emerson. "I thought that Christ used miracles to convince, and that Christians today appealed to these miracles as the strongest evidence of Bible authenticity."

"Christ repeatedly appealed to fulfilled prophecy as evidence His contemporaries might accept," answered Mr. Dare. "Fulfilled prophecy is especially adapted as a test, for we are nineteen hundred years from the latest Bible book and thirty-three hundred years from the first.

"You may look back at the miracles of the Bible through the mists of time and declare them improbable, if not impossible, but the opposite is true of prophecy. Those beholding His miracles were convinced by them, while many of the prophecies that were unfulfilled were apparently opposed to all reason and probability, and might, in those days, have been made an excuse for rejecting Christ.

"Obviously, miracles performed twenty-five hundred years ago cannot be seen now, so they are often flatly denied. A prediction, however, made twenty-five hundred years ago, that contrary to all analogy and a stumbling block at the time, but that was recently fulfilled, is evidence even more convincing than a miracle—such a fulfilled prediction is the greatest of all miracles, and so admitted by the skeptic Hume.

"Other evidence can be falsified, changed, lost; memory may fail, conflicting statements may cloud the issue; passion, self-interest, dishonesty, any one of a thousand things, may impair proofs. But prophecy relates to history, and history is recorded fact.

"How was God, through all the shifting interests of the world, the engrossing allurements of the new demands of each new generation, the dying interest in that which is gone, and the eagerness for that which is to come—how was God to give those of us who live today unimpeachable testimony of events so remote as three thousand years ago? How was He to satisfy a reasonable demand for proof? And above all, how was God to give increasing and strengthening proof as we get further and further from the event itself?

"God has devised an absolutely new method of proving His Word, one that cannot be gainsaid, that cannot be counterfeited, that has no duplicate in all the history of the world, that increases in power with each passing year, that is stronger each tomorrow than it was yesterday."

David Dare paused and looked searchingly at his large audience. No one took the occasion to press in with remarks, so he continued:

"This strange method of eternally authenticating His Word compels the ruin of empires long dead, the mutation of states, the obliteration of nations and civilizations, to witness to the truth of His Word.

"All the places famous in antiquity—Egypt, Syria, Phoenicia, Arabia, Tyre, Sidon, Idumea, Palestine, Babylon, Assyria, Nineveh, Judea, Rome, and many other countries—are witnesses that do not forget, do not contradict, and, though dead these many centuries, rise to testify. When put in the jury box, they cannot be confused. Some of the oldest of them have been before the jury thirty-three hundred years, the youngest, two thousand. They are now on the stand, fresh and potent, bearing their testimony with far greater fullness and accuracy than at any former time.

"The ages do not detract from, but add to, their testimony. Minute cross-examination serves only to increase the swelling volume of evidence. No counterproof has yet been attempted."

Mr. Emerson arose. All eyes turned his way. Mr. Dare waited for him to speak.

"Suppose we did disprove many of the Bible prophecies—what would we accomplish by such disproof?" he asked.

"The Bible stakes everything on its ability to foretell the future. If the Bible claim to make genuine predictions is true, it is a miracle of foresight far beyond the ability of human sagacity to discern or to calculate, and is the highest evidence that can be given of the supernatural knowledge of the prophet.

"God claims to be the only one able to foretell the future. He says in Isaiah 46:9, 10: 'I am God, and there is none like me, declaring the end from the beginning, and from ancient times the things that are not yet done.'

"The ability to foretell is the seal of God's deity which He claims cannot be counterfeited. The Bible challenges others everywhere to foretell the future: 'Who, as I, . . . shall declare . . . the things that are coming, and that shall come to pass, let them declare' [Isa. 44:7, ASV].

"But this is by no means all. Such strong claims are not casually made. Have you skeptics a cause to present? Hear Isaiah 41:21-23: 'Produce your cause, saith Jehovah; bring forth your strong reasons.' Now, what are the strong reasons? Let us read on: 'Declare unto us what shall happen: declare ye . . . things to come. Declare the things that are to come hereafter, that we may know that ye are gods' [ASV]."

"Has your Bible fulfilled these conditions?" asked Mr. Emerson. "I do not mean in a vague manner, but in a clear and definite way?"

" 'Have I not declared unto thee of old, and showed it?' asks God [in Isaiah 44:8, ASV]. And then He says, 'Ye are My witnesses,' " returned David Dare.

"You, yes, even you, Mr. Emerson, and the rest of the skeptics in this audience, are witnesses to the accuracy of prophecies made many centuries ago."

Mr. Emerson shot to his feet. "Do you mean that you are going to prove your prophecy thesis by *us*?" he asked in great amazement.

"That is exactly what I do mean," smiled the speaker, evidently enjoying the intense surprise of the audience.

"But we don't believe your Bible; we think its predictions

the sheerest kind of foolishness, and yet you say you are going to prove by us the very thing we don't believe?" Mr. Emerson was incredulous.

Lucile leaned over to whisper to her brother, "He has an interesting line, all right; he's got Dad excited !"

George smiled. "Yes, and Dad is not the only one excited. Look around," he whispered back.

She looked. Every face in the audience was alight with eager curiosity; eyes sparkled with interest.

"The fact that you are unbelievers, that you are unwilling witnesses, makes your testimony all the more valuable," continued Mr. Dare as Mr. Emerson sat down. "God declared twenty-five hundred years ago that He is going to prove His Word by the very ones who say they doubt His Word. This is a daring statement. Yet it is by your evidence that Bible prophecies will be proved.

"While science has solved many strange problems, and seems to be almost supernatural, it has not brought us one whit nearer to penetrating the future than were the ancients. Human beings can as easily pluck the stars from the Milky Way as they can wrest from the future its secrets. We are utterly unable to foresee even dimly the events of tomorrow. Before us is a black, impenetrable wall of uncertainty. We can guess, we can hope, but we cannot know.

"But if the future has been read; if centuries ago numerous predictions, so varied and so minute that they cover well-known nations and extend over thousands of years—if such predictions have been made so as to preclude all possibility of wresting the facts to fit the prophecy; if skeptics themselves admit the accuracy of the fulfillment, and can offer no explanation; and if you here are witnesses to this fulfillment of prophecies made more than twenty-five hundred years ago, how can you doubt that some wisdom more than human foretold the events that have come to pass?

"What shall we say of a large Book filled with predictions of events overspreading all time and all nations, events utterly disconnected from any facts existing at the time of their utterance, events totally unlike anything ever known and the reverse of all experience, in all respects improbable and often seemingly impossible, events entering into the life of the world in all its phases? A series of hundreds of such events were demonstrably predicted ages before fulfillment, and not one of them has gone contrary, as might well be the case with so many predictions. The proof of their fulfillment is now existing in tangible form before your eyes. What shall we say of such a Book?

"In the verses I have quoted, God has challenged anyone and everyone on earth to a prophecy contest, and will abide by the result. God claims to be the only one who can look into the future and make predictions. He tells us He has done this, and offers these prophecies as the one great proof of His Godhead.

"Is it a fact that no other book in existence makes such a claim? Can you produce any other book claiming to contain predictions looking hundreds of years, or even tens of years, into the future? If you know of any in any language, produce it. God Himself challenges you.

"Skeptics have gone to great pains and expense to disprove the Bible. I will tell you two very simple, effective, and final methods of shattering the Bible to atoms: First, just disprove the prophecies; second, produce some other book containing real prophecies. God says neither can be done. To do either will blast forever all confidence in the Bible as the Word of God. Why have unbelievers never done this? Does anyone here claim that this has been done? Will anyone here attempt to do it?"

David Dare paused for the reply he felt sure would follow. There was an uneasy stir among the audience. Mr. Emerson arose and spoke:

"Bring on your prophecies, and we will see what we can do. You have made some large, not to say preposterous, claims for them. Let us now have your evidence."

"We are more than pleased to present it," replied Mr. Dare.

CHAPTER 3

THE TEST BEGINS

THE applause that greeted Mr. Emerson's demand indicated the anxiety of the audience to hear the evidence. David Dare, Bible in hand, stepped to the edge of the platform and proceeded with his talk:

"For two thousand years Tyre grew in importance until she was mistress of the sea as was Babylon of the land. She was the commercial center of the world. Carthage, the rival of Rome, was only a colony of Tyre—Tyre, the beautiful, the rich, the learned, into which flowed the fine gold of Tarshish, the precious stones of Aram, the spirited horses of Armenia, the beautiful ivories of Damascus, the fine linen of Egypt, the flocks of Arabia, the rich perfumes of Sheba, the slaves of Javan.

"In short, Tyre was the New York of Asia. Ships from all nations anchored in her harbor and their passengers bartered in her streets.

"While Tyre was at the height of her glory and power, while it would seem she must stand forever, along came Ezekiel, who prophesied about 590 B.C.: 'They shall destroy the walls of Tyrus, and break down her towers: I will also scrape her dust from her, and make her like the top of a rock. It shall be a place for the spreading of nets in the midst of the sea: for I have spoken it, saith the Lord God: . . . and they shall lay thy stones and thy timber and thy dust in the midst of the water . . . . And I will make thee like the top of a rock: thou shalt be a place to spread nets upon; thou shalt be built no more: for I the Lord have spoken it, saith the Lord God' [Eze. 26:4-14].

"Immediately after the giving of the prophecy, Nebuchadnezzar besieged Tyre and, after thirteen years of effort, took the city and destroyed it, wreaking fearful vengeance on buildings and people."

Here an auditor jumped to his feet. Without waiting for Mr. Dare to recognize him, without giving his name, he plunged into a tirade against the Bible and the speaker.

The place was soon in an uproar. Men arose all over the room. Shouts of "Sit down," "Put him out," "Speak up," were heard above the murmuring.

One of the sponsors of the meeting, standing with blanched face, white with anger, raised his voice during a moment of silence in denunciation of the interrupter, who stood glaring defiance.

It looked as if a roughhouse were inevitable. Mr. Emerson shook his head in disapproval of the loud, coarse tactics of his brother unbeliever. Lucile's eyes sparkled with excitement as she gripped her brother's hand. Mrs. Emerson looked frightened.

Just as the meeting seemed to be getting out of control, David Dare raised his hand impressively, and in a calm, loud, clear voice began to speak. The contestants ceased their wrangling and listened. Turning to the sponsor of the meetings and manager of the hall, he said:

"Mr. Marshall, will you please sit down?" Mr. Marshall dropped as if shot, surprised chagrin on his features. "Have you forgotten our agreement? I consented to this series with the distinct understanding that I, and I alone, am to reply to all interruptions from the floor. I am advertised to reply. Presumably people come to hear the person advertised." There was a murmur of approval. Mr. Dare turned to the man who had caused the commotion. He was still standing in a rather belligerent attitude. All others had seated themselves.

"Let me make it plain that only skeptics may interrupt in these meetings. But they are freely urged to do this. It is their guaranteed right. The advertisement inviting them to interrupt was not a rhetorical gesture, but an honest invitation to honest doubters to come here and voice their questions in a gentlemanly, serious, frank manner.

"Now, sir, please repeat your question."

The Emerson family looked at each other in pleased surprise. "Well, this is something new in public meetings," whispered father to son. "The doubter is at last being given preference in a meeting conducted by Christians, but apparently such generosity is not unanimous."

The large audience applauded the stand taken by Mr. Dare.

They saw that it was not merely an empty pretense, but a vital part of the speaker's plan.

The objector was plainly confused. He was of the belligerent type, at home in a rough-and-tumble verbal battle—an iconoclast of the street corner. His courage evaporated as opposition ceased.

"Go ahead; speak up," urged the crowd, sensing his confusion. The lecturer smiled encouragement, and added: "You need have no fears; you will not be interrupted again."

"All I wanted to say was that you cannot prove that the prophecy was written before Nebuchadnezzar's time. According to your own statement, Ezekiel was contemporary with the king." He sat down abruptly.

His statement was now courteous both in wording and in manner, where before it had been both blasphemous and insulting. There was a sigh of relief from most of the audience, but of disappointment from some who relished a "scene."

"True," agreed David Dare. "While personally I believe that the prediction was made before Nebuchadnezzar besieged Tyre, I shall not refer merely to that siege. Though the prophecy began with the king of Babylon's siege, its predictions looked more than two thousand years into the future, as we shall see.

"Observe that while the ruins of the old city remained after Nebuchadnezzar had finished with it, the prophecy declared that the timbers and rocks and even the very dust should be cast into the sea, leaving a bare rock to be used for spreading nets.

"This prediction was not fulfilled by this king of Babylon, and it seemed improbable that it ever would be fulfilled; for if Nebuchadnezzar, in his anger, had taken full vengeance, and had not thought of this, who was likely to care enough about the ruins of a deserted city to be so violently destructive? It would be the very frenzy of madness. But meanwhile there stood the prophetic words, awaiting fulfillment.

"Two and a half centuries passed, and still the ruins stood, a challenge to the accuracy of prophecy. Then through the East the fame of Alexander the Great sent a thrill of terror. He marched swiftly to attack new Tyre, 332 B.C. Reaching the shore, he saw the city he had come to take, with a half mile of water surging between them; for it was built upon an island. Alexander's plan of attack was speedily formed and vigorously executed. He took the walls, towers, timbers, and ruined houses and palaces of the ancient Tyre, and with them built a solid causeway to the island city. So great was the demand for material that the very dust was scraped from the site and laid in the sea."

When the original objector made no movement, Mr. Emerson stood up to speak.

"I grant the statements you have made concerning Tyre are true, but what of it? It will be impossible for you to prove that the supposed prophecy was written before the events it describes. At this great distance from the events, three or four centuries is a small matter. Your argument is far from conclusive, and I for one believe the book of Ezekiel was written after Alexander's time."

Lecturer Dare smiled in reply: "Perhaps the fact that the events fit the prediction has much to do with your conclusion."

"And perhaps the fact that history verifies Ezekiel's prediction," retorted Emerson, "has much to do with your belief that the prediction was written first. My assumption has as much foundation as yours, and is more reasonable."

"Good shot, Dad," encouraged Lucile in a stage whisper, as the audience laughed.

"You overlook three great difficulties in your view," replied Mr. Dare. "First, the *Encyclopedia Britannica,* fourteenth edition, Volume IX, pages 13, 14, under the article 'Ezekiel,' is emphatic in stating that the book of Ezekiel was written 586-450 B.C., and this is the extreme critical view. Thus, according to the skeptical version, the prophecy is still one hundred eighteen years antecedent to the event. But we will pass to the second difficulty.

"When you claim Ezekiel pretends to foretell what in reality was written after the event it professes to predict, you make a book of otherwise high moral teaching a most vicious book, dealing in deception of the basest sort.

"But, Mr. Emerson, while you create these two difficulties for yourself, there is still a third inherent in your position that no skeptic can remove.

"I will admit, for the sake of the argument, that the book was written whenever you desire, say 330 B.C. Even you cannot claim a later date." Mr. Emerson nodded agreement.

"Perhaps you forget there are other particulars in the prediction besides destruction. In some prophecies the cities were to be destroyed and rebuilt. Such was the fate of Jerusalem, which still exists.

"The third difficulty of your view is that old Tyre was to be built no more. This divine sentence of judgment has been a challenge down the centuries to every unbeliever on earth. God has had a challenge sounding for twenty centuries, daring you and every other skeptic to rebuild this city and thus disprove His Word."

"I never heard of such a thing," gasped Mr. Emerson in surprise. "Are you serious?"

"Certainly," replied David Dare, "never more so. I will next tell you how to disprove the Bible."

CHAPTER 4

HOW TO DISPROVE THE BIBLE

David Dare's statement that he would tell unbelievers how to disprove the Bible startled some of his listeners. A few Christians were shocked, and said so. Unbelievers were amazed.

Mr. Emerson arose and spoke: "Do you mean to tell us that you admit the Bible can be disproved?"

"On the contrary, I do not believe any part of the Bible can be disproved," smiled Mr. Dare.

"But you said you would show us how to disprove it," insisted Mr. Emerson.

"And I will."

"Your statements sound contradictory, but let's hear what you have to say."

"God Himself has not only dared you to disprove His predictions, but has taken the pains to tell you how. Tyre has continued a daily defiance to every unbeliever. 'Thou shalt be built no more: for I the Lord have spoken it,' says the prophecy. Read it for yourself in Ezekiel 26:14. The reason it cannot be rebuilt is here given. Here is a test that God has set for the boasting unbeliever—the simple one of rebuilding a city. To do that one thing would disprove the Bible.

"And this is not asking an unheard-of thing. Many cities in the past have been rebuilt; even Rome rose again, after Nero had it burned to furnish him with poetic inspiration.

"That a city can be built in a surprisingly short time, by a few determined men, was proved recently when a marsh was transformed by one man into the modern city of Longview, Washington, in two years. I visited the city personally, and marveled at the amazing feat.

"A dollar each from the unbelievers in England and America would be sufficient to rebuild Tyre, and thus blast forever the reputation of the Bible as a truth-telling book. Why not form an infidel colony on the site of old Tyre, go into the fishing business in a modern manner, and there, in defiance of the prophecy, dare to answer God's challenge, 'Thou shalt be built no more: for I the Lord have spoken it'?

"The site is inhabitable; for ten million gallons of water daily gush from the springs, and fertile fields stretch clear to the distant mountains.

"Knowing that there are millions of determined doubters who write numberless books to disprove the Bible, how did any prophet have the breathtaking daring to utter such a defiant prophecy? For two thousand years no skeptic has dared say the prediction is untrue. In fact, Volney, the French skeptic, tells of visiting this spot and observing fishermen drying their nets on the rocks, just as the prophet said they would [*Travels,* Vol. II, p. 212]. Every year, every day, every minute that Tyre has remained in utter ruin it has disproved the emphatic declaration of skeptics that all Bible predictions are vague, or were made after the events that they foretell took place.

"'A good guess,' you say. But that is not a sufficient answer. It is especially lame in view of the fact that no person outside of the Bible ever made a solitary correct forecast covering hundreds of years concerning any city on earth. How is it that only Bible writers are able to 'guess' with perfect accuracy two thousand years into the future?"

Mr. Emerson stood up to reply: "It would be natural for a writer, looking upon a ruined city, to assume, hence to predict, that it would never again be inhabited."

"Such an assumption, however natural," replied Mr. Dare, "would have plunged the prophet immediately into serious difficulty.

"To illustrate: Ezekiel turned his attention to Tyre's still more ancient sister city, only thirty miles distant. For centuries it had been declining in power, while Tyre was still glorying in the splendor of its heyday. Accepting your view of the date of Ezekiel adds strength to our contention, for while Sidon was still in a state of decay it was taken by Artaxerxes Ochus, king of Persia, in 351 B.C., and destroyed!

"Now, according to your theory, Mr. Emerson, Ezekiel was

written still later, at least after Alexander's time. So if the prophet were judging by appearances in 330 B.C., as you claim he did judge, he would have pronounced complete oblivion as the inevitable fate of Sidon, for nothing seemed more certain than its utter eradication. But Sidon still remains, even now possessing ten thousand population. Let us read the words of the prophet Ezekiel [Eze. 28:20-23]:

"'The word of Jehovah came unto me, saying, Son of man, set thy face toward Sidon, and prophesy against it, and say, Thus saith the Lord Jehovah: Behold, I am against thee, O Sidon. . . . For I will send pestilence into her, and blood into her streets; and the wounded shall fall in the midst of her, with the sword upon her on every side.'

"Observe that the judgment on Sidon was not utter extinction like that on Tyre, but only blood in her streets, wounded in her midst, the sword on every side. In spite of the fact that no other city on earth, with the possible exception of Jerusalem, has had so much suffering, has been so often destroyed and rebuilt, Sidon has continued an uninterrupted existence down to the present minute.

"Now, suppose Ezekiel had said that both Tyre and Sidon were to be destroyed and were to be built no more. Then every one of the ten thousand inhabitants of Sidon would be a living proof of the falsity of the prophecy.

"Suppose, further, that the prophet had said Tyre was to live, but would undergo great suffering, while Sidon was to be utterly destroyed and never be rebuilt; how derisive the skeptic would rightly be of the Bible claim to predictive accuracy!

"How did it happen that the prophet was exactly right in both cases? How is it that the city that never has been rebuilt is the city of which this fact was foretold, and that the city that has continued to exist with agelong suffering is that which the prophet foresaw would continue in existence to the end of time?

"Having explained this to your satisfaction, a still harder question remains to be answered. Sidon, like many other ancient cities, might have sunk into insignificance, so that in its utter misery and defenselessness it could have offered no resistance to even a feeble enemy, and would have tempted no one's cupidity. How did Ezekiel know that, in spite of many terrible experiences, it would continue a place of strength that, age after age, would be fought for, and passed on, wet with blood, from one conqueror to another?"

Mr. Emerson replied: "These two cities were well known and powerful, but at the time of the predictions there were indications of the fate that was to befall them. The predictions turn out to be fairly accurate; but you cannot establish your thesis that the Bible is true on so slim a basis."

"Certainly not, and I do not claim to," responded Mr. Dare. "A prophecy to meet any test you desire to make can easily be produced. You claim that Tyre and Sidon had already to some extent indicated in themselves their fate. We'll take a city of which this cannot possibly be said.

"Out of a score of such forecasts, notice two sentences about Ashkelon, a city hardly less famous than the two we have just considered. Ashkelon shall be 'a desolation' [Zeph. 2:4]; 'Ashkelon shall not be inhabited' [Zech. 9:5].

"This city was founded 1800 B.C., and was in the height of its power about the time of Christ. So you cannot claim that at the time of the prediction its impending fate was apparent to the observer. But how about it now?

"Let me quote from the fourteenth edition of the *Encyclopedia Britannica,* Volume II, page 544: 'Now a desolate site on the seacoast twelve miles north of Gaza. . . . Protruding from this sand-swept terrain, shattered columns and the remnants of ruined buildings and broken walls bear ample testimony to a past magnificence. . . . The country around is fertile. Vines, olives, and a variety of fruit trees flourish.'

"Observe that this world-recognized authority, in describing the present condition of Ashkelon, uses the very word of the prophet—'desolate.' The prophet saw twenty-five hundred years ago what the historian now sees, and both use the same word to describe the final condition of that city. But to quote further from the same authority:

"Ashkelon 'was the birthplace of Herod the Great, who adorned it with fine buildings. During the Roman period it was a noted center of Hellenic scholarship. It became also the seat of a bishopric. From 104 B.C. for four and a half centuries it was an oppiduni liberum of the Roman Empire.'

"Thus on any theory of biblical composition the city grew in importance for hundreds of years after the prediction.

"In A.D. 636 it passed to the Arabs. During the Crusades it was the key to southwest Palestine. Baldwin III captured it after six months' siege in 1153. It was thus still a very powerful city fifteen centuries after the prophet foretold its destruction. During the next hundred years its history was a bloody one. Finally, in 1270, Sultan Beibars destroyed its fortifications and blocked its harbor with stones. Thus for six hundred sixty years the lofty towers of Ashkelon have lain scattered on the ground, giving a picture of desolation, and the ruins within its walls do not shelter a solitary human being.

"But suppose Ashkelon were, like Sidon, a flourishing city; suppose the predictions had been transposed. How eagerly would unbelievers seize upon the fact! And if it were a fact, it should be used. The Bible says: 'Never disdain prophetic revelations but test them all' [1 Thess. 5:20, 21, Moffatt].

"You do the disdaining, but not the testing. Here are three cities. The prophets foretold their condition exactly as they are today. However you choose to account for it, the fact remains that these prophecies are true."

Mr. Emerson took this occasion to speak: "You have picked out three cities. Surely, if the Lord is the author of predictions, He tells us something about whole nations as well. And the predictions should be given at a time when it would seem impossible for the forecast to come true, and should reach to the present time."

"Your suggestions are reasonable. Out of several countries that meet your test, we will select the oldest country in the world—Egypt."

CHAPTER 5

Egypt Confounds the Unbeliever

You have all admitted," said David Dare as Mr. Emerson sat down, "that Tyre, Sidon, and Ashkelon are today exactly as the Bible prophets said they would be. But you are unwilling to admit, or are not convinced, that this uncanny foresight is the result of any supernatural gift.

"Yet you know that while the past and present yield their treasures, tomorrow is mockingly silent. Hope may fondly picture what the future holds; despair may dread it; sagacity may judge what it ought to be—but the unaided mind of man has never penetrated the heavy, thick curtain of the future.

"Let us always bear in mind, during these talks, how circumscribed is the most remarkable foresight of the most astute statesman.

"The stream of history may flow uniformly for a dozen centuries, until shrewd thinkers reason from analogy that the course of events will continue thus indefinitely. Then, unforeseen, a single man, like Muhammad or Luther, may change the whole course of history; or like Watt or Edison or the Wright brothers, may revolutionize civilization.

"The prophecies I have already given are positive, accurate, and truthful to the minutest detail; but we have only entered the doorway of the great prophetic temple.

"When Isaiah, Jeremiah, and Ezekiel lived, Egypt was then so ancient that she boasted a longer unbroken line of kings than did any other nation. To Ezekiel, the settling of Egypt was as ancient as the beginning of the Christian religion is to us.

"The prophets of his day, 600 B.C., knew Egypt as the granary of the world, eminent in science, in the arts, in luxury and magnificence, a leader of civilization. For many centuries those artificial mountains, the justly famed pyramids of Egypt, had stood as proud sentinels of a proud country of many splendors.

"Like its own monuments, Egypt seemed to bid defiance to

the tooth of time. At the fire that burned on her hearth, all nations had kindled the lamp of knowledge. She had the unity, pose, and calm majesty of conscious power, the grandeur of great age. To the eye of the natural man, be he scientist or philosopher, there appeared on the horizon of the future no faintest cloud to threaten the peace and power of Egypt.

"Nevertheless, at a time when all other men, judging by analogy, would have predicted for her practically unending prosperity, Isaiah [Isa. 19] and Ezekiel [Eze. 29 and 30] foretold many amazing things concerning her, reaching more than two thousand years beyond their death!

"When you get home, read these chapters carefully, as every verse is literally packed with meaning. I shall not take time to quote more than a few of the more outstanding statements.

"In a few words, Ezekiel foretold history that has taken twenty-five hundred years to fulfill and would take several volumes to record. I quote Ezekiel 29:14, 15; 30:6, 7; 32:15; 30:12, 13:

" 'They shall be there a base kingdom. It shall be the basest of the kingdoms; neither shall it exalt itself any more above the nations: for I will diminish them, that they shall no more rule over the nations.' 'The pride of her power shall come down. . . . And they shall be desolate in the midst of the countries that are desolate, and her cities shall be in the midst of the cities that are wasted.' 'I shall make the land of Egypt desolate, and the country shall be destitute of that whereof it was full.' 'I will . . . sell the land into the hand of the wicked: and I will make the land waste, and all that is therein, by the hand of strangers: I the Lord have spoken it. . . . And there shall be no more a prince of the land of Egypt.'

"Every phrase of the verses I have quoted is surcharged with meaning. The doom of Edom and Chaldea and Babylon was utter extinction; but not so the fate of Egypt. The inexorable decree was one of continual baseness and decline. It was to continue a nation, but it was no longer to rule. On the contrary, it was to be ruled by cruel strangers.

"We have only to consider the condition of Egypt six hundred years later to see that this prophecy could not have been the result of mere human foresight. In the time of Christ there was nothing to indicate that the day of Egypt was past forever. She was still very powerful.

"Augustus, after the defeat of Antony, found so great wealth in Egypt that out of it he paid all the arrears of his army and all the debts he had incurred during the war. Even after he had spoiled Egypt at will, she still appeared to him so formidable that he was afraid to entrust her rulership to any man of power, lest a rival to himself arise. So he gave the government to Cornelius Gallus, a person of very low extraction. He denied Alexandria a municipal council, and declared all Egyptians incapable of being admitted to the senate at Rome.

"And for six hundred years more, Alexandria continued the first city in the Roman Empire in rank, commerce, and prosperity. Certainly the skeptic of that day might have read the prophecy of Ezekiel with a mocking smile of derision, and taunted the believing Christian with his unfulfilled prophecy. True, part of the prediction had been fulfilled, but the desolation of Egypt seemed as remote as when the prophecy had been uttered more than a thousand years previously.

"A hundred years later Egypt was still so powerful that the Muslim hordes, though arrogant with unchecked victory, hesitated to attack it. When Romulus and Remus founded Rome, Egypt was then nearly two thousand years old. Rome waxed powerful, conquered the world, including Egypt, and was, in turn, conquered by the barbarian hosts of the north. But still Egypt continued powerful, rich, and populous. The Arabs finally decided to attack her. The memorable siege of Alexandria lasted fourteen months, during which the Arabs lost twenty-three thousand men. And then her capture was the result of internal treachery. The sight of the city's magnificence and wealth filled the conquerors with amazement.

"The burning of the famous Alexandrian library was a world calamity. Its destruction supplied the Arabs with fuel for six months. The wealth of Alexandria was an indication of the riches and strength of the whole Egyptian nation. It would have been impossible for the Arabs, despite their prowess as warriors, to take the land and to retain it, had not the people, groaning under the cruel oppression of their Greek masters, thrown themselves into the arms of the invaders.

"While the prophecy may seem slow of fulfillment, it has been certain. The decline, though gradual, has been continuous. Let the infidel pens of Volney and Gibbon tell the story.

"'Such is the state of Egypt,' says Volney, in his *Travels,* Volume I, pages 74, 103, 110, 193: 'Deprived two thousand three hundred years ago of her natural proprietors, she has seen her fertile fields successively a prey to the Persians, the Macedonians, the Romans, the Greeks, the Arabs, the Georgians, and at length, the race of Tartars distinguished by the name of Ottoman Turks. The Mamelukes, purchased as slaves, and introduced as soldiers, soon usurped the power, and elected a leader.

"'If their first establishment was a singular event, their continuance is not less extraordinary. They are replaced by slaves brought from their original country. Their system of oppression is methodical. Everything the traveler sees or hears reminds him he is in the country of slavery and tyranny.'

"And Gibbon tells us that 'a more unjust and absurd constitution cannot be devised than that which condemns the natives of a country to perpetual servitude, under the arbitrary dominion of strangers and slaves. Yet such has been the state of Egypt above five hundred years' [*Decline and Fall of the Roman Empire,* chap. 59].

"Thus do infidel historians witness to the fact that Egypt has declined steadily, until during the past five hundred years and more she has been exactly what the prophet said she would become, 'the basest of the kingdoms,' ruled 'by the hand of strangers.'

"And note this: not until modern times could the amazing accuracy of this prediction be appreciated. The more facts we have with which to test this prophecy, the more true it shows itself. Is there anyone here who claims Egypt to be different than it is pictured in Ezekiel? How then do you account for the fact that Ezekiel is right, which of necessity you admit?"

Mr. Emerson stood up again: "The writer had observed that in time nations are conquered and become the servants of their masters. He had seen Babylonia and Assyria, as well as smaller kingdoms, pass into the hands of others. Though Egypt was old and still powerful, he reasoned that she, too, would in time suffer the fate of the others."

"But, Mr. Emerson, you overlook a vital point in your argument: Egypt did not suffer the fate of the others. Babylonia, Assyria, and other nations about were destroyed utterly. Had Ezekiel been predicting by analogy, he would have said that Egypt would suffer the same fate as the nations that had already been overthrown.

"Now, just suppose that Ezekiel had said that Egypt would, like Babylon and Chaldea, be utterly destroyed, how jubilant would be the skeptics, and how eager to point out the fact that the Egypt of today has many populous cities and a varied population that numbers into the millions. But does the unbeliever attempt to show us a single prophecy concerning Egypt that has failed?"

"Have you given all of them?" asked Mr. Emerson.

"I have only touched the edges of the subject. I will call your attention to only two or three more marvelous predictions concerning Egypt," replied Mr. Dare.

"I realize that to some here it may seem as if studying the history of ancient Egypt is a dull and unsatisfactory way of seeking God. I do it because God Himself has told us that if we study these prophecies faithfully, we shall be directed to Him.

"After all, it should interest us intensely to learn whether there actually did exist twenty-five hundred years ago persons who could look ahead to our time and tell exactly the fate of the cities and nations of their day.

"I now direct your attention to Ezekiel 30:13: 'Thus saith the Lord Jehovah: I will also destroy the idols, and I will cause the images to cease from Memphis' [ASV].

"Observe that these words are specifically the words of 'the Lord Jehovah.' If the thing predicted did not come to pass, there would be no alibi.

"Now, it is a strange fact that Memphis, founded by Menes, was known as 'the great temple city of Egypt.' A more unlikely fate could hardly be imagined than the destruction of the idols and images of Memphis, because

"1. The climate of Egypt, where it never rains, keeps in a state of perfect preservation for thousands of years whatever is buried in its soil.

"2. In all other cities of Egypt, whether in ruins or now flourishing, idols and images are found in superabundance.

34

Thebes, former capital of Egypt, though in ruins while Memphis was still in splendor, has them in abundance.

"3. At the birth of Christ, six hundred years after the prophet lived, the predicted ruin seemed more impossible still, for Memphis was large and populous, Alexandria being the only Egyptian city that exceeded it in size.

"4. And twelve hundred years after the prophet lived, Memphis was the residence of the governor of Egypt. So you see it was impossible for the prophet to have written this prophecy after the event.

"5. And in the thirteenth century Abdul-Latif, an Arabian traveler, tells of the 'wonderful works which confound the intellect, and to describe which the most eloquent man would labor in vain.'

"Thus, eighteen hundred years after the prediction it was still unfulfilled, and—"

Mr. Emerson stood up, and David Dare stopped abruptly, waiting for him to speak.

"Mr. Dare," he said, "I observe that your prophecies are a long, long time fulfilling. A thousand to two thousand years are necessary for your prophecies to prove themselves. Now, given enough time, any prophecy concerning the destruction of a city or nation must be fulfilled. So, since these prophecies were uttered admittedly about twenty-five hundred years ago, there has been ample time for them to be fulfilled. There is nothing so very miraculous about it."

A ripple of applause greeted Mr. Emerson as he sat down. Lucile leaned over and patted her father's hand approvingly, while George nodded in agreement.

"I was hoping, Mr. Emerson," replied Mr. Dare, as the applause died down, "that you would make such an observation. Your very argument is proof that you admit the fulfillment; that you do not claim the prediction was written after the event, nor that the facts have been juggled to fit the prophecy.

"The audience will please observe that if the fulfillment of the prediction is near the date of the prediction, it is at once claimed that the prophecy must have been made after the date of the fulfillment. And if the fulfillment is two thousand years after the prediction, the explanation then is that any prediction will eventually be fulfilled, given time enough.

"But unfortunately for this theory, some prophecies already mentioned and others to be produced cannot be explained in this easy manner, and—"

"Can you give any convincing example?" asked Mr. Emerson.

"Memphis, the very city we have been considering, is a good example, for time did not destroy the idols and images of other Egyptian cities equally old. But listen to these words from Miss Amelia B. Edwards, Egyptologist, in her book, *A Thousand Miles up the Nile*: 'And this is all that remains of Memphis, eldest of cities: a few rubbish heaps, a dozen or so of broken statues, and a name! . . . Where are the stately ruins that even in the Middle Ages extended over a space estimated at half a day's journey in every direction? One can hardly believe that a great city ever flourished on this spot, or understand how it should have been effaced so utterly' [pp. 97-99].

"But let us suppose that all that was necessary to fulfillment was time. Now turn your attention to Ezekiel 30:12: 'I . . . will sell the land into the hand of evil men' [ASV].

"This certainly denotes unresisting surrender into the hand of an enemy, just as slaves were sold. The slave has no rights, the wicked no mercy.

"Volney, the French skeptic who traveled all over this country, calls Egypt 'the country of slavery and tyranny.' Malte-Brun, another traveler, writes of 'the arbitrary sway of the ruffian masters of Egypt.'

"The history of Egypt for the past eighteen hundred years is but an amazing commentary on the words, 'I will . . . sell the land into the hand of the wicked.' The impress of that terrible hand is everywhere seen."

Mr. Emerson interposed: "It would be a safe prediction to say evil men would govern. Nearly always rulers of the past, especially conquerors, were evil men."

"True," replied Mr. Dare. "I am glad you admit the truth of the prediction, whatever your explanation. However, in this connection consider another prediction in the same verse: 'I will make the land desolate, and all that is therein, by the hand of strangers' [ASV].

"Never once in all the past twenty-five hundred years has Egypt been under the rule of her own prince, but always, without even the solitary exception to prove the rule, she has been a subject nation, ruled by strangers—Persians, Greeks, Romans, Byzantine Greeks, Saracens, Turks, French, and British—strangers, always strangers, as predicted.

"Now, here is a prophecy that time would tend to defeat. For other subject nations have thrown off the yoke, grown in power, and finally made their former masters serve them. How did the prophet know that the Egyptians would never regain control of their government?

"But this is not all. In the next verse the prophet ventures further: 'There shall be no more a prince from the land of Egypt.'*

"This, too, was a prediction that each succeeding year rendered less likely to continue true, for if a nation remained worth governing, there was likely to arise in Egypt, as in other conquered nations, a strong man from among themselves who would overthrow the foreign rulers and regain the throne. This happened again and again in Roman history, but never once in Egyptian history. Further, consider the fact that never elsewhere in the history of the world has any nation been subject so long without once governing herself. How did the prophet know all this? For to predict it he must have known it.

"Does anyone here claim that the prophecies concerning Egypt have failed at any point during the past twenty-five hundred years? Consider the strength of the skeptics' position if Mr. Emerson could show concerning Egypt what he can concerning Rome, that though conquered, she threw off the yoke and ruled herself, or had her own prince occasionally.

"But he cannot. On the contrary, you have to admit the accurate fulfillment of the predictions; and when I press you for a reasonable explanation of the strange phenomena, various weak and failing solutions are given.

"Robert G. Ingersoll, the famous skeptic, and Henry Ward Beecher, the great preacher, were friends. In the study of the famous minister was an elaborate celestial globe. On the surface, in delicate workmanship, were raised figures of the constellations, and the stars that compose them. The globe struck Ingersoll's fancy. He turned it round and round in frank admiration.

" 'That is just what I want,' he said finally; 'who made it?'

" 'Who made it, do you ask, Colonel?' repeated Beecher in mock astonishment. 'Who made this globe? Why, nobody, of course. It just happened.'

"When confronted with the facts of fulfillment of prophecy, you are compelled to admit the fulfillment, but when driven from one insufficient explanation to another, your final explanation is 'It just happened.'

"The fact that it never has happened outside of the Bible, you do not attempt to explain. But you do say you will not accept any explanation that has the supernatural in it.

"Is that a reasonable attitude, one that dignifies a thinker? Surely the only attitude philosophers may rightly claim is to proclaim themselves willing to follow the evidence, no matter if it leads them to conclusions contrary to those previously held.

"At our next meeting we will consider the most all-embracing prophecy in the Bible, outlining the history of all nations of the earth, beginning twenty-five hundred years ago and reaching to the present moment, yourselves being the judges."

---

* King Fouad I, the present king of Egypt, is not by descent an Egyptian, but an Albanian. He is one of the sons of the late Khedive Ismail Pasha, who in turn was the second of three sons of Ibrahim, a grandson of Mehemet Ah. Mehemet Ah is thus the founder of the present royal house of Egypt. He was born at Kavala, a small seaport on the frontier of Thrace and Macedonia. His father, an Albanian, was an aga, a small yeoman farmer, and he himself began life as a petty official and trader in tobacco. By a compromise between the powers of Europe, Mehemet Ah was made a hereditary ruler of Egypt. So Egypt is in reality under foreign rule, and to this day, as the Word of God foretold, has been without a native prince.

CHAPTER 6

THE DARING OF DANIEL

"You stated, Mr. Emerson, that any prediction, given time enough, would eventually be fulfilled," said David Dare, after the large audience had been called to order by the chairman.

"You have given up the attempt to show that all prophecy was given after the event, and now go to the opposite extreme and make time the solvent of your difficulty. We shall see how completely time, instead of fulfilling, would refute the prediction of a prophet of the Old Testament.

"The story of the decline and fall of the Roman Empire was first written, not by Edward Gibbon the skeptic in the eighteenth century A.D., but by Daniel the prophet in the sixth century B.C. And Gibbon the skeptic used six large volumes in telling us in detail how accurate were the predictions of Daniel the prophet."

Mr. Emerson arose, amazement in his face, excitement in his manner. "Do you claim that Daniel wrote the book attributed to him in the sixth century B.C.? Why," and here Mr. Emerson turned to the audience and spread his hands wide in a gesture of helpless astonishment, "why, in all the range of Bible criticism nothing is more widely accepted or more easily proved than that the book of Daniel was not written by Daniel at all, but was written by some unknown author about 168 B.C."

"I am well aware of the fact, Mr. Emerson," replied Mr. Dare, "that against the book of Daniel the heavy artillery of the critics has been directed since Celsus of the third century discovered that the accuracy of these predictions could not be denied. In chapters 2 and 7 are such clear predictions, giving in vivid outline the whole history of the world, beginning with Babylon and reaching to the present moment, that the most skeptical have been hard put to it to account for them without admitting supernatural knowledge on the part of the prophet.

"Infidels seem to think that if only they can show that

Daniel never wrote a word of the book, and that it was composed by some unknown person about 168 B.C., its power will be broken and its prophecies vitiated. But for my purpose I will accept the latest date contended for by anyone, and care not who wrote it.

"It is not my purpose to go into the marvelous details of the prophecies of Daniel 2 and 7. It would take a whole series of lectures to cover the subject as it deserves. I plan to develop only one point.

"No matter what the opinion of doubters concerning the date and authorship of Daniel, they admit it teaches that, beginning with Babylon, there will be just four universal world powers—four and no more—to the end of time.

"If, as I believe, Daniel lived in 600 B.C., he foretold the rise and fall of the three empires to follow Babylon—a marvelous prediction in itself. It is to deprive Daniel of the honor of having done this that skeptics have desperately contended that the book of Daniel was written in 168 B.C.—after Rome had acquired rulership.

"Then, if it is true, as the skeptics assert, that the writer of Daniel lived in 168, he had knowledge of the fact that in a period of only four hundred years, Babylon, Medo-Persia, Greece, and Rome had ruled the world in succession. Babylon fell in 538 B.C., conquered by Cyrus, king of Medo-Persia. At Arbela in 331 B.C., Alexander wrested the world empire from Medo-Persia. The Roman victory at Pydna, June 22, 168 B.C., marked the final establishment of the Roman world rule. Thus in three hundred seventy years, 538 B.C. to 168 B.C., four universal empires bore sway.

"In view of this fact the predictions of Daniel 2 and 7, if written in 168 B.C., are fully as remarkable as if they were written in 600 B.C. Despite the fact that four world kingdoms existed in four hundred years, think of the amazing daring of a man who would have the temerity to predict that in all future history there would never be another world power! How preposterous, how contrary to all analogy, to all previous history, to the wildest imagination, was such a prediction!

"While there were four universal empires in four centuries, there have not been, as analogy would teach, twenty more universal empires in the twenty succeeding centuries. On the contrary, there has not been even one! How do you account for this amazing fact?

"Daniel knew this, for he foretold it. But how did he know it? Here is a case in which each succeeding century would make more strange the fulfillment, because it was directly contrary to the trend of history.

"If experience had been asked to guess the secrets of the future, the reply given by the wise of earth of that day would certainly have been that the revolutions of the past would be repeated again and again in the coming two thousand years, as in the past four hundred years; for then, as now, it was believed that 'history repeats itself.'

"As the Babylonian Empire was conquered by the Persian, the Persian by the Grecian, the Grecian by the Roman, so would every observant thinker also expect the Roman Empire as certainly to be succeeded by some other world power. But was this the fact? Every schoolboy knows that Rome was the last world kingdom. Someone else knew it before Rome became a ruling power! Again I ask, Where did he get this knowledge?

"Unbelievers realize how unaccountably marvelous were the predictions of Daniel if they were written while Babylon still ruled the world. And they think they have removed the difficulty by bringing the composition of the prophecy down to the time Rome took control.

"But instead of solving the problem, they have only placed themselves in a dilemma, and to me it is immaterial which horn of the dilemma they take, the problem remains as great either way. Whether the book of Daniel was written about 600 B.C. or 168 B.C., leaves the problem of prediction unsolved."

"I don't see how you make that out," interrupted Mr. Emerson. "For if Daniel was not written until after the world empires had come and gone, certainly you lose the benefit of claiming a prophet who foretold the rise and fall of those powers."

"That is granted," smiled David Dare. "But let us consider the matter both ways for a moment. If Daniel was written about 600 B.C., it is conceded by skeptics everywhere that the predictions are too marvelous to be explained away easily. But you skeptics overlook the fact that if your contention that it was written about 168 B.C. be granted, you introduce another marvel equal to the marvel you eliminate by putting the writing later."

"I still do not see how that can be," said Mr. Emerson.

"I'll make it clear," said Mr. Dare. "By putting the composition of Daniel in 168 B.C., you place the four great universal kingdoms in the past instead of in the future. You thus give the writer the analogy of immediately past history by which to judge the future. He has seen four universal kingdoms arise in four hundred years. But in making his prediction, he goes absolutely contrary to every fact of past history. This is what no philosopher, using all the information at hand, would ever dream of doing. Hence, it is clear that the writer of Daniel had some other source of information than that accessible to anyone else.

"On the other hand, if the book of Daniel was written about 600 B.C., its author did not have available any evidence of one universal kingdom followed by another, for the nations before that date, while powerful, were not universal. Thus in 600 B.C. the precedents of history were unsettled, while in 168 B.C. they were settled. The dating of Daniel in 168 B.C. removes one difficulty only to add another, equally unsolvable by human wisdom.

"But this is by no means all. Let us look at the picture Daniel draws of today.

"Imagine," said the lecturer, "the bewilderment of the believer of 100 B.C. who read the prediction of Daniel that there would never be another world dominion throughout all the ages to come, except that of the kingdom of God; and imagine the derisive sneers of the skeptics of that day over such an absurd prediction.

"But today skeptic and believer alike look back through the ages to Daniel's time, and they both agree there has been no other. Read any history written by anyone. But in particular, read the great history written by one of the greatest unbelievers of all time—Gibbon's *Decline and Fall of the Roman Empire*—and you will see that this 'immortal' work is but an unwitting commentary on the uncanny accuracy of Daniel.

"Let Gibbon the infidel tell how the fierce, rude warriors of the north poured like a flood against the Western Empire in the fifth century; but though they conquered Rome, world dominion was denied them.

"Let him tell how in the seventh century the Arab hordes, sweeping out of the deserts, assaulted the empire on the east. They assaulted also on the west. For a time it seemed as if the caliphs might rule from the throne of the Caesars. Tartars and Turks swept in power and fury over the East. They knocked loudly at the gates of the West, and mankind trembled lest they rule the world; but dominion was denied them.

"However, the dream of world dominion did not pass with them. The pages of history, for the past two thousand years, though wet with the blood of untold millions, record in unvarying sequence the repeated failure of all attempts to establish a world power.

"The attempts to break the prophecy of Daniel went merrily on. The mighty Charlemagne, the swift Charles XII of Sweden, the resistless, eagle-eyed Napoleon, the ambitious Miser, and many other Goliaths of war have hoped to wear the toga of the mighty Caesars, but always their endeavors have ended in failure.

"But not only did the prophet foretell that there would never be another universal kingdom after the fourth—he predicted the breaking up of the fourth into a number of smaller nations, which were to continue to exist, with exceptions noted by the prophet himself, to the end of time.

"Now, can you imagine the predicament the Christian would be in today if, somewhere down the ages, after the fall of Rome, a world dominion like that of Rome had thrust itself athwart the stream of history? Suppose some all-powerful Alexander of the Middle Ages had conquered all the known nations of the world, and cemented them into one mighty empire subject to his sovereign will—what could I say? I pause to inquire if any skeptic here can produce any such failure of prophecy.

"Every great king or powerful warrior assumed that someone was of necessity going to be a world ruler, and asked why he should not be the one? And if just one had succeeded, what an irrefutable argument against the truth of prophecy the skeptic would have! God challenged the unbeliever twenty five centuries ago either to make prophecies of his own or to break one of His. As yet, no one has done either. The plain historical facts, as related by themselves, make their own criticisms absurd.

"Each fulfillment, taken by itself, is a strong point in favor of divine wisdom on the part of the prophet, but each additional fulfillment increases the strength of the evidence, not by addition, but by multiplication.

"Every Jew you meet is a miracle. This will be proved in our next lecture."

CHAPTER 7

EVERY JEW A MIRACLE

I approach this subject with a feeling of profound awe," said David Dare, after the crowd had been called to order by Dr. Morely. "Nowhere in all the world is there anything so strange, so wonderful, so sad, as the Jew. He is the most pathetic, most unique being on earth.

"Vast ruins, moldering palaces, broken sculptures, shattered and marred by the violence and vengeance of barbarians, are all that remain of Rome, mightiest of kingdoms.

"The palaces of the Caesars lie desolate. The kingdom of Rome has sunk into oblivion, the names of its rulers are forgotten, or remembered only for their merited infamy. The iron kingdom, as foretold by Daniel, has been shattered and divided, and has no successor.

"But the Jewish nation, whose downfall Rome in the heyday of its power accomplished, whose leader was slain, whose city was destroyed, whose Temple was annihilated, whose children Rome sold as slaves—that nation still lives and thrives and multiplies on earth.

"Rome has long since passed away, but the Jewish people remain. Centuries before Rome was founded, the Jews were a powerful nation. The history of Rome—the mightiest of kingdoms—was only a parenthesis in that of the Jews.

"Strange to observe, the nations that were enemies of the Jews have perished. But the Jews, oppressed, banished, enslaved, and spoiled wherever they were driven, have survived and have overspread the earth. Of all the nations around Judea, Persia alone remains a kingdom. And it furnishes food for thought to observe that it was the Persians who restored the Jews from the Babylonian captivity.

"In Leviticus and Deuteronomy, Moses clearly outlines the political and religious history of the Jews for thirty-four hundred years—from 1500 B.C. to this present moment."

"But you cannot prove Moses wrote these predictions," interrupted Mr. Emerson. "In fact, it is generally conceded that the Pentateuch was not written until 800-600 B.C. instead of 1500 B.C., a matter of 700 to 900 years' difference."

"For our purpose," smiled Mr. Dare, "it is immaterial whether the books credited to Moses were written 1500 B.C. or 100 B.C. So I'll cheerfully accept your latest date. But that will not solve your difficulty. I will ask you, Mr. Emerson, to read Leviticus 26:33, 36, 37, and 44; also Deuteronomy 28:25."

"Certainly," he replied. He opened his Bible as indicated, and read in a strong, clear voice: " 'I will scatter you among the heathen, and will draw out a sword after you: and your land shall be desolate, and your cities waste.' 'And upon them that are left alive of you I will send a faintness into their hearts in the lands of their enemies.' 'And ye shall have no power to stand before your enemies.' 'And yet for all of that, when they be in the land of their enemies, I will not cast them away, neither will I abhor them, to destroy them utterly.' 'The Lord shall cause thee to be smitten before thine enemies: thou shalt go out one way against them, and flee seven ways before them: and shalt be removed into all the kingdoms of the earth.' "

"Thank you, Mr. Emerson. The scriptures just read are a very few that bear on the subject. Please read the following in addition, for they are important and illuminating: Jeremiah 15:4; 16:13; 9:15, 16; 24:9, 10; 15:7; Ezekiel 5:10; 7:19; 12:15; Amos 9:4, 9; Jeremiah 8:3; Hosea 9:17; Isaiah 6:10-12; Jeremiah 31:10; 46:27, 28; Hosea 3:4, 5; and above all, the whole of Deuteronomy 28.

"Now, here is another instance in which time, instead of making the problem more simple, makes it more difficult, for we can understand how a people might for a hundred years mingle with other nations and remain distinct, but when this mingling extends to twenty-five hundred years, how shall we account for that nation's remaining distinct all that time? The history of the world presents nothing else like it. Scores of other nations have meanwhile risen up, remained distinct for a while, and then become entirely lost in the great mass of humankind.

"Look at our own country. Millions from other nations pour

in. For two or three generations they preserve their nationality, but after that it is lost.

"But not so the Jews. They are in every nation, as predicted, and everywhere a distinct people. They are indeed an astonishment. The Jews preserve all the characteristics that they had many centuries ago. They have done what no other people on earth have ever done—they have successfully resisted all the customs of society, all the powers of persecution, all the powerful influences that tend to drive them toward amalgamation with other nations. The children of Abraham are as distinct in religion, customs, and physiognomy as they were three thousand years ago. How do you account for this?"

"The bloodstream of this particular people," said Mr. Emerson, "was absolutely pure, kept pure because they were forbidden to intermarry. Hence racial peculiarities have persisted."

"True, they were forbidden to intermarry," replied Mr. Dare. "Your explanation, instead of explaining, adds another difficulty, that of explaining how Moses knew the Jews would obey that mandate thousands of years later.

"Here is a case in which every nation in the world has had a part in fulfilling the prophecies of the Bible, for there is not a nation in all the world where the Jews have not gone, and not one where they have not been oppressed in accordance with the prediction.

"Can you point out a solitary nation that has received the Jews with open arms? If you could find a half dozen such, what a case against the Bible the skeptic would have. But how amazingly remarkable it is that the Jews have been thus oppressed in every nation, and are the only nation in all history to be thus oppressed.

"Another remarkable thing about it all is the fact that the records telling of their shame are handed down to us by the very people we would naturally expect would want them destroyed. No, there is no other instance of such remarkable fidelity to truth in all history.

"As foretold by Moses, the Jews have literally been 'rooted' out of their land [Deut. 29:25, 28]. Not only that, but God says, 'I will bring the land into desolation; and your enemies that dwell therein shall be astonished at it' [Lev. 26:32].

"Please observe that while the Jews were to be deprived of

their land, scattered to every part of the world, and Palestine lay in ruins, still their enemies were to 'dwell' in it. Could any prediction seem more improbable?

"Dean Stanley, in his *Syria and Palestine,* says that 'Palestine above all other countries in the world is a land of ruins' [p.117]. Is it not a strange fact that a land so filled with ruins should be inhabited? Or being inhabited, that the ruins should not have been utilized or removed? But the inspired writer foresaw this fact, and you and I are compelled to admit the marvelous correspondence of fact to prediction.

"Though ruined, desolate, bereft of her own people, Palestine was nevertheless to be preeminently a land of pilgrimages, for Moses tells of 'the foreigner that shall come from a far land' [Deut. 29:22, ASV]. And is this not true today? Is there any other spot on earth to which so many pilgrims journey? Not one! More than half a hundred languages are spoken in the city of Jerusalem alone.

"'I will draw out a sword after you,' declares Jehovah, speaking to the Jews [see Lev. 26:33, ASV]. The history of this people has been one long, bloody commentary on the uncanny accuracy of this prediction.

"In A.D. 70 approximately 2 million of them were killed, starved to death, or sold into a slavery worse than death in A. D. 70 More than a half million more were slaughtered by the Romans sixty years later. The history of the Israelites has been but the slaughter of a nation, continuing for nineteen centuries—the sword drawn out after them.

"But let the words of the historian Milman tell the story: 'No fanatic monk set the populace in commotion, no public calamity took place, no atrocious or extravagant report was propagated, but it fell upon the heads of this unhappy caste. In Germany the black plague raged in all its fury; and wild superstition charged the Jews, as elsewhere, with causing and aggravating the misery, and themselves enjoying a guilty comparative security amid the universal desolation.

"'The same dark stories were industriously propagated, readily believed, and ferociously avenged, of fountains poisoned, children crucified. . . . Still, persecuted in one city, they fled to another, and thus spread over the whole [country]. Oppressed by nobles, anathematized by the clergy, hated as rivals in trade by burghers in commercial cities, despised and abhorred by the populace, their existence is known by the chronicle of their massacres [*History of the Jews,* Vol. III, pp. 222, 223].

"Exiles from their own land, without central government, without ruler, scattered over the whole earth, they have nevertheless been preserved.'Massacred by thousands, yet springing up again from their undying stock, the Jews appear at all times and in all regions. Their perpetuity, their national immortality, is at once the most curious problem to the political inquirer, to the religious man a subject of profound and awful admiration' [*ibid.,* Vol. II, pp. 298, 299].

"That this people, very limited in extent and power in comparison with the great monarchies of the then-known world, should, after having been actually rooted out of their own land by their conquerors, and scattered among the nations, have withstood nineteen hundred years of unremitting persecution, and still retain their individuality of race, is the most astounding and unexplainable fact in the history of nations.

"And as marvelous an enigma is the further fact that all this was foretold in detail, as skeptics admit, at least two thousand five hundred, and I believe three thousand four hundred, years ago. How did Moses and Ezekiel and Jeremiah know all these things thousands of years before they came to pass? Will anyone here maintain that these Bible writers were mistaken in what they said would happen to the Jews?

"Let us suppose that the Jews, like the Amalekites, or Philistines, or Moabites, or Assyrians, or Chaldeans, or Egyptians, or Romans, or other contemporary nations, had been utterly destroyed; or that they had amalgamated with other nations; or had remained, as have the Persians, in their own land; or had been dispersed among the nations and gradually disappeared; or had been secluded in a single region, but remained united—with what glee would skeptics have produced these very prophecies as proof of a fallible Bible!

"Through all the centuries, the evidence presented by the everyday history of the Jew has served only to pile proof on proof of the truth of the prophetic predictions. These prophecies are plain, precise, and circumstantial; their fulfillment is literal, complete, and undeniable."

CHAPTER 8

Skeptics Compelled
to Witness for the Bible

A slight ripple of applause greeted David Dare's appearance on the platform at the next meeting. He smiled his acknowledgment, and began:

"Look at mighty Babylon in the heyday of her glory. Here was a city that seemed destined to endure forever. The 'golden city' had grown more and more powerful, until it was now the wonder of the ancient world.

"She drew her stores from no foreign country. She invented an alphabet; worked out problems of arithmetic; invented implements for measuring time; conceived the plan of building enormous structures with the poorest of all materials—clay; discovered the art of polishing, boring, and engraving gems; knew how to reproduce faithfully the outlines of human and animal forms; attained high perfection in textile fabrics; studied successfully the motions of the heavenly bodies; conceived of grammar as a science; elaborated a system of law; saw the value of exact chronology. In almost every branch of science she made a beginning. Much of the art and learning of Greece came from Babylon.

"No, never had the world seen such a city. Its great rampart walls towered upward two hundred feet, and on top several chariots could race abreast. Gleaming in the sun, its lofty palaces and temple towers stabbed the sky above the towering walls and thrilled approaching travelers while they were yet miles away.

"Here was the magnificent temple of Belus; and here were the world-famous hanging gardens, piled in successive terraces.

"Babylon was not only mistress of the world, but she reposed securely in the midst of the most fertile region of the whole known world. The country was so astoundingly fruitful that Herodotus feared he would be taken for a liar if he related what he had actually seen of the amazing fertility of the soil here."

Mr. Dare ceased speaking as Mr. Emerson arose.

"Everybody here knows these facts about Babylon," he said. "We came here to have infidelity refuted, not to listen to a lecture on the greatness of Babylon, no matter how edifying."

"I am glad you admit these facts," smiled the lecturer. "And they most certainly do bear on my subject, for even before Babylon had become ruler of the world, a prophet wrote in a book and proclaimed openly that 'Babylon, the glory of kingdoms, the beauty of the Chaldeans' pride, shall be as when God overthrew Sodom and Gomorrah' [Isa. 13:19, ASV].

"A simple statement, that, but one that disproves utterly your contention that Bible predictions are like Delphic oracles, so that no matter what happens the event may be interpreted to be a fulfillment of the prediction.

"In effect the dating prophet says: 'I see the greatness of Babylon; I observe her apparently impregnable walls. I know that she is mighty and powerful, the greatest city the world has ever seen. Nevertheless, this apparently imperishable city of Babylon shall be as completely obliterated as were Sodom and Gomorrah.'

"Looking back over the history of Babylon as we now know it, can anyone here in so few words, or in any words, better express the present condition of the former mistress of the world?

"But God saw you, Mr. Emerson, and all the other doubters of today, and He caused the Bible prophet to word His prophecy so plainly that you could never justly accuse Him of double-meaning predictions. So He went on to say: 'It shall never be inhabited' [verse 20]. And for fear some hardheaded doubter might suggest that He meant something else, He added, 'Neither shall it be dwelt in from generation to generation: neither shall the Arabian pitch tent there; neither shall shepherds make their flocks to lie down there' [verse 20, ASV].

"Now, who can make anything ambiguous out of that? Is there anyone here who does not understand these words?

"But this is by no means all. Even though the words were plain, the predictions seem to be so utterly impossible that most readers would decide the writer to be either mistaken or insane.

But Jeremiah comes to the support of Isaiah, and the meaning of what these prophets wrote is clear indeed, whatever people of any nation or clime or tongue may think of their message.

51

"'Thou [Babylon] shalt be desolate forever' [Jer. 51:26]. 'Babylon shall become heaps, a dwelling-place for jackals, an astonishment, and a hissing, without inhabitant' [verse 37, ASV].

Mr. Emerson indicated that he wished to speak.

"To be forewarned is to be forearmed," he said. "After such messages of impending destruction, the people would certainly have been prepared, if they knew of these predictions."

"Yes, the people of Babylon might have exerted their strength and ingenuity to ward off their fate, but it would have availed them nothing, for 'though Babylon should mount up to heaven, and though she should fortify the height of her strength, yet from me shall destroyers come unto her, saith Jehovah' [Jer. 51:53, ASV].

"Is Babylon inhabited today? Is any human being dwelling there? Not even one? Where is the man who will deny the truth of these predictions? Now, Mr. Emerson, I ask you directly: Are these predictions true? Have they been fulfilled?"

"Come, Dad, speak up," urged Lucile. Then in a whisper aside to George:

"Looks as if he has Dad really stuck."

"Does look bad," George admitted.

"Do you claim these predictions are wrong, Mr. Emerson?" Mr. Dare spoke again.

"Of course every schoolboy knows Babylon has been uninhabited for centuries," came the answer. "But, Mr. Dare, how do we know that these predictions were not written after the destruction of Babylon, and dated before?" Mr. Emerson sat down amid a slight murmur of approval.

"Would you affirm these predictions were made after Christ's time?" asked Mr. Dare.

"Of course not," replied Mr. Emerson, "for everybody knows they were included in the Septuagint."

"True, and so the crux of the whole question is When were the prophecies of Isaiah and Jeremiah written? As they were included in the Septuagint, they must have been written before that translation was made. When was the Septuagint made?"

"About 200 B.C.," answered Mr. Emerson.

"True," replied Mr. Dare, "and for the purposes of this discussion, I will accept 200 B.C. as the date of the composition of these predictions concerning Babylon. Will you accept 200 B.C. as the nearest possible date for the giving of these predictions, Mr. Emerson?"

"Yes, certainly."

"Does anyone here contend for a still later date?" asked the speaker, pausing for reply. No one spoke. "Then do you all agree that these prophecies I have quoted could not possibly have been given later than 200 B.C.?" Again he paused, questioning. The audience nodded agreement.

"Then we are a unit as to two things: First, that the predictions are true; and second, that they could not have been made later than 200 B.C."

Mr. Emerson spoke again: "If you admit, Mr. Dare, that the predictions you have quoted were not written before 200 B.C., you have given your case away—your cause is lost."

David Dare smiled. "On the contrary, the cause of infidelity is thereby made extremely difficult."

"How so?"

"Because of the astonishing fact that these prophecies were not completely fulfilled, according to the admission of the most critical skeptics, until hundreds of years after Christ was crucified."

Gasps of surprise were heard all over the room. George looked at his sister with raised eyebrows. She smiled back, happy, for she scented a real contest. Mrs. Emerson looked annoyed. Mr. Emerson seemed startled. The audience leaned forward in interested expectancy.

"Well, his argument begins to sound conclusive," Lucile whispered to George.

"Just wait; Dad isn't through yet."

"I should hope not!" she smiled.

"But this is by no means all," went on Mr. Dare. "Not only was the fall of Babylon foretold by these prophets, but they saw and described fallen Babylon as it is at this moment—at least two thousand years since they made their amazing prophecies.

"Read thoughtfully the following: Isaiah 13; 14:4-24; 21:1-10; 47:1-11; Jeremiah 25:12-14, 50, 51. There is enough detail in these marvelous predictions to fill a book. Those who think these predictions ambiguous, raise the hand."

No hands went up.

"Now those who think the predictions plain and distinct, raise the hand."

This time a sea of hands were lifted. "It looks almost unanimous," he remarked.

"Since it was admittedly centuries after the predictions were written before they were fulfilled, no one claims that the prophecies were written after the events predicted took place. Does anyone here make such a claim? If so, please raise the hand." Mr. Dare waited. There was no response.

"All right. Let us get this clear now. Those who not only admit that the predictions are clear and definite, but also that they were made before the events foretold, raise the right hand." A sea of hands went up, quickly this time.

Lucile and George looked around, glanced at each other, and smiled.

"Looks as if Mr. Dare wins the first heat," ventured Lucile.

Mr. Emerson looked perplexed. "First time I've seen Dad so perturbed," responded George. Then he leaned over and spoke to his parent:

"Is this audience largely Christian, Father?"

"No," said Mr. Emerson, puckering his brows, "and that is why I am at a loss to understand this vote. I know many of the people here, and they are as skeptical as I am, yet they are voting in the affirmative."

"Could you vote any other way?" asked George.

"Not the way he worded his question, but we are not through yet. There are—" He broke off as David Dare began to speak.

"Since the facts I have mentioned are admitted by all of you, how do you, Mr. Emerson, explain their remarkable fulfillment?"

"Those prophets were austere religionists," answered Mr. Emerson, "who saw the wickedness of great cities, and to them Babylon was the symbol of evil; and as they believed God more powerful than the cities, they believed He would overthrow them. So they actually predicted what they so earnestly believed and desired, and not because they had the slightest foreknowledge given from any supernatural source."

Lucile nodded as her father sat down. "Not so bad, Dad," she whispered.

"Clever, and quite plausible at first thought," smiled Mr. Dare. "But let us consider a few facts. If the date 200 B.C. is accepted as the approximate date of the predictions, Rome was then twice as old as New York is now, and grew more powerful than Babylon. But the prophets never predicted the destruction of Rome. It still exists after 2,600 years. Yet these 'religious enthusiasts' had as much reason to desire the extinction of Rome as of Babylon.

"The answer given by Mr. Emerson comes perilously near to admitting divine aid. He does base his explanation on a sort of 'religious enthusiasm' which was so keen that it gave the prophets an uncanny foresight into the future. But there seems to be more to it than just the religious frenzy born of pessimism and misanthropy.

"Even if, in a sort of religious frenzy, Isaiah and Jeremiah had guessed right about the destruction of Babylon, how can you account for the details of their predictions?

"That such a land, peopled with the world's most highly civilized inhabitants, the 'golden city,' situated in the most fertile spot of the known world, should become a wild, desolate, seared, wholly unproductive and uninhabited desert was from a human viewpoint utterly impossible. Not only had such a calamity never befallen any country at that time, but such a calamity has never yet taken place in Europe, China, or America—not anywhere but in Babylon—to the present day!

"Great Babylon, the city of Baal, the capital and wonder of the world, fought against Jerusalem, a giant against a pygmy, and Jerusalem became the slave of the giant. But both Babylon and its people have vanished like a dream of the night, while Jerusalem and its people still remain. These facts, predicted by the prophets, need some explaining other than to say the predictions are merely the vaporings of 'religious enthusiasts.'

"'Without inhabitant,' said the prophets. How true, how weirdly, uncannily true! But this is not all. The positions of the world's most important cities are usually so well chosen, so rich in natural advantages, that population clings to them. Dwindle and decay as they may, some collection of human dwellings still occupies a portion of the original site. Damascus, Jerusalem, Athens, Rome, Antioch, Alexandria, Byzantium, Sidon—all have remained continuously cities of consequence from the time of their foundation thousands of years ago to the present. But it remained for the greatest, richest of all to sink into utter oblivion. How do you account for that, and for the fact that this was all foretold so long ago?"

As no one replied, the speaker continued:

"And we are by no means through. In Isaiah 13:20 we read that 'neither shall the Arabian pitch tent there.' Now, how did Isaiah know that the Arabian would continue to exist after Babylon had become dust?

"While a few humble Arabs lived in tents about Babylon twenty-five hundred years ago, the Babylonians were the haughty rulers of the world. The utter extinction of the ruling race was foretold, and all the world knows there is not a solitary living Babylonian. But the prophet also said in effect: 'While the most powerful race on earth will become extinct, together with their world-ruling city, still this small, insignificant, nomadic race of Arabs will continue on and on for two thousand years, long after this proud city has crumbled to ruins and its very site is almost forgotten.'

"How did Isaiah know that the Arabs would continue to live near Babylon? Yet the prophecy clearly implies this. Since they were a wandering race, it would be logical to suppose that in time they would either leave the vicinity of such a place as we now know Babylon to be, or would themselves become extinct. But how did Isaiah know they would remain about Babylon's ruins for two thousand years; that they would be there today? Imagine the jeering sarcasm of skeptics if there were not an Arab within a thousand miles of Babylon! And what Homeric mirth would be theirs if all Arabs had become as extinct as the dodo, before Babylon sank into oblivion!

"How did Isaiah know that the Arabs would continue to live in tents? In the ruins of Babylon was ample material to build many villages by the simple process of transporting it to more favorable spots. But Arabs dwell in tents to this day. The probabilities were all against this. Of no other people has this been true in the world's history.

"And how did Isaiah know that the Arabs would not make use of the ruins of Babylon for shelter?

"Many explorers and excavators of recent years report that it is impossible to get Arabs to remain on the site of this ancient city overnight. Captain Mignan was accompanied by six Arabs completely armed, but he 'could not induce them to remain toward night, from apprehension of evil spirits. It is impossible to eradicate this idea from the minds of these people,' *Travels,* p. 235. Yet, as everyone knows, the Arabs are fearless fighters, dangerous warriors."

Mr. Emerson interrupted here. "You make quite a point out of the little prediction about the Arabs. Some of your statements would be equally true of gypsies. They are a nomadic people, living largely in tents."

"The prophecy concerning the Arabs," explained David Dare, "is so obviously true that no one, not even you, Mr. Emerson, can deny the accuracy of the prediction. And the remarkable correspondence of the facts today to the ancient forecast moves the skeptics to bring in the gypsies to lessen the force of the prophecy.

"But the case of the gypsies has no bearing. In the first place, they did not come into existence until long years after the time of Isaiah. And in the second place, they do wander everywhere. They have never remained, as have the Arabs, for many hundreds of years near the ruins of ancient cities. So, even if the gypsies had lived in the time of Isaiah, his prophecy would not have been true of them. It is still a fact that the prophecy about the Arabs is amazingly unique in every particular, and every passing day serves only to strengthen its force."

Mr. Emerson indicated his desire to speak. "I grant that you have brought forward a number of remarkable facts to make a case for prophecy, but surely you do not expect a few unusual coincidences or amazing guesses to convince us? Have you not about exhausted your evidence from Babylon?"

"On the contrary, I have only touched the edges of the abundance of confirmation. There are more than a hundred particulars in the prophecy, each one of which furnishes remarkable evidence of prophetic foresight. All taken together, they would fill a large book. I shall take time to mention but two more.

"In Jeremiah 51:58 we are told that 'the broad walls of Babylon shall be utterly broken' [ASV]. For centuries after this sentence of destruction was issued against these, the strongest walls ever built about a city, they continued to be numbered among the seven wonders of the world."

"There is nothing so remarkable about either this prediction or its fulfillment," interrupted Mr. Emerson. "The prophet, as you call him, who would predict the destruction of the city would naturally predict the destruction of the walls."

"You forget," replied David Dare, "that all ancient cities had walls, and that other cities with walls not nearly so strong as those of Babylon have been destroyed, but their walls remain in a remarkable state of preservation. However, all I desire to prove by this is that Jeremiah was right. Suppose, for instance, that the walls were standing today in grim defiance of the prophet's words. The Great Wall of China, not nearly so strong, is, though older, still standing. If you, Mr. Emerson, could tell this audience that you had seen Babylon's magnificent walls jutting, like the pyramids of Egypt, above the surrounding plains, what a blow it would be against the Bible. But you cannot do this, for the prophet was right, as usual.

"Finally, we read: 'Chaldea shall be a spoil: all that spoil her shall be satisfied, saith the Lord' [Jer. 50:10]. 'Come against her from the utmost border, open her storehouses: . . . and destroy her utterly' [verse 26]. 'A sword is upon her treasures; and they shall be robbed' [verse 37]. 'Abundant in treasures, thine end is come' [Jer. 51:13].

"There are two particulars to be noted: First, there is an implication in the little word 'all' that Babylon and the other cities of Chaldea would often be despoiled. Nothing like this was predicted of Tyre or of Nineveh or of many other cities and countries doomed by prophetic wrath to destruction.

"Second, how did the prophet know there would be riches enough to tempt and satisfy spoiler after spoiler? Tyre was one of the richest cities of earth, but after one spoliation by Nebuchadnezzar nothing was left to tempt another conqueror.

"But the teeming riches of Babylon and the surrounding country bade defiance to the greedy ravages of successive plunderers. No sooner did a fresh horde of conquerors pillage the country than another army was preparing to fight them for the booty, and loot the country anew.

"Cyrus took huge treasures; Xerxes and his army took $150 million in gold alone, besides other rich plunder. Then came Alexander, but so far from finding Babylon's wealth exhausted, he gave from her stores $50 to every soldier in his vast army, and kept immense wealth for himself. Continuously for two hundred years after the death of Alexander, the Parthians ravaged this country, and then came the Romans from a long distance, according to the prediction, for the same purpose.

"One would think that after several hundred years of plundering, not much of value could be left. Gibbon, the skeptic, is the best commentator on this prophecy, because an unwitting one. He tells of numerous expeditions, covering a period of several hundred years, gathered for the purpose of sacking Babylon's ruins and the ruins of adjoining cities. He says that the spoil was such as might be expected from the riches and luxury of an Oriental camp. And later, when the Romans, under Heraclius, ravaged Chaldea, Gibbon tells us that 'though much of the treasure had been removed, . . . the remaining wealth appears to have exceeded their hopes, and even to have satiated their avarice' [*Decline and Fall of the Roman Empire,* Vol. IV, p. 480].

"Again, Gibbon has painted the joy of still another band of conquerors in 636, hundreds of years after the prophecy was uttered: 'The naked robbers of the desert were suddenly enriched beyond the measure of their hope or knowledge. Each chamber revealed a new treasure secreted with art, or ostentatiously displayed; the gold and silver, the various wardrobes and precious furniture, surpassed (says Abulfeda) the estimate of fancy or numbers; and another historian defines the untold and almost infinite mass, by the fabulous computation of three thousands of thousands of thousands of pieces of gold' [Vol. V, p. 180]. And this after centuries of ravaging, looting, pillaging by the huge armies and mighty conquerors of earth! And rich treasures are still being found right up to the present moment, as you well know.

"But nowhere else on earth have the conquerors of empires gone back again and again for hundreds of years for loot, and come away laden beyond the dreams of avarice, regardless of the immense booty carried off by the previous despoilers. Yet the prophet foretold what the skeptic Gibbon recorded as history.

"Although the picture of ruined Babylon was given so many years ago, there are few spots on earth of which we have so clear and true a picture. The historian writing now cannot so faithfully delineate conditions as did Isaiah, Ezekiel, and Jeremiah more than two millennia ago.

"You may believe they made clever guesses, or that the marvelous truth of all their forecasts was coincidence only, if you can; but your credulity or faith in that convenient solvent of difficulties, coincidences, arouses my wonder.

"And next I will tell you of an infidel ruler who was determined to defeat prophecy, who used the resources of a vast kingdom and the genius of his favorite commander in an attempt to accomplish his purpose."

CHAPTER 9

INFIDEL RULER TRIES TO BREAK PROPHECY

David Dare found the hall crowded when he arrived. He chatted a few minutes with friends, then met Dr. Morely, and together they went to the platform. As he arose to speak, there was rather an unusual ovation.

Mr. Dare smiled acknowledgment. "I see you are interested in the subject announced for today," he remarked. "To me it is gratifying to see someone with the courage of his convictions and willing to do more than talk about them. Most doubters never go beyond the talking stage.

"After all, it should be an easy matter for infidels to disprove the Bible if they were half as much in earnest as they would have us believe. They need only rebuild old Tyre, or Babylon, or Nineveh; for God has said that these cities will never again have inhabitants. And He challenged the world to disprove His words.

"If unbelievers would inhabit only one of these doomed cities, they would no longer be compelled to argue the question of Bible prophecy, for they themselves would be the living disproof of its truth."

"But that is a fantastic idea, and an absurd and unreasonable thing to ask of skeptics," protested Mr. Emerson.

"I agree with Mr. Dare, Dad," whispered Lucile, as he sat down. "If doubters set such great store by their skepticism, let them venture something on it, or keep still. Certainly the believers venture everything—their property and even their lives; the skeptics, not even a few dollars. Yes, the speaker is right."

"The thought of actually trying to disprove a prophecy," replied Mr. Dare, "is not so fantastic. It is just what ought to occur to the logical mind. It did occur to one determined doubter.

"There lived about 300 A.D. a learned man who read the words of Jesus in Luke 21:24: 'Jerusalem shall be trodden down of the Gentiles, until the times of the Gentiles be fulfilled' [ASV]. He had once been a Christian, so he knew the predictions. He made up his mind that Jerusalem should be trodden underfoot by the Israelites instead of by the Gentiles.

"This man also knew that the Bible foretold the utter destruction of the Jewish Temple and its services, that the Jews were to be scattered to all nations of the earth, and that Christianity was to go to 'every nation, and kindred, and tongue, and people.'

"He was determined to overthrow Christianity, not by killing its adherents, which had been tried by his predecessors for two hundred fifty years, and had served only to increase its followers, but by the more effective method of shattering the prophecies. Thus he would prove Jesus a liar. And he had the power, if anyone ever had, for he was Julian, emperor of Rome, with an immense army and the wealth and power of the civilized world at his command."

"Aren't you assuming a great deal when you assert that Julian had no other purpose in mind than to disprove the Bible?" asked Mr. Emerson.

"That he intended to stage a contest between himself and God, that he consciously planned to disprove prophecy, is stated by a writer as infidelic as Julian himself—Edward Gibbon, the world's accepted authority on that period, in chapter 23 of his famous history. Rather than paraphrase, I will read Gibbon's account:

"Julian 'embraced the extraordinary design of rebuilding the temple at Jerusalem. In a public epistle to the nation or community of the Jews, dispersed through the provinces, he pities their misfortunes, condemns their oppressors, praises their constancy, declares himself their gracious protector. . . . They deserved the friendship of Julian by their implacable hatred of the Christian name. . . .

"'After the final destruction of the temple by the arms of Titus and Hadrian, a plowshare was drawn over the consecrated ground, as a sign of perpetual interdiction. . . .

"'The vain and ambitious mind of Julian might aspire to restore the ancient glory of the temple of Jerusalem. As the Christians were firmly persuaded that a sentence of everlasting destruction had been pronounced against the whole fabric of the Mosaic law, the imperial sophist would have converted the success of his undertaking into a specious argument against the faith of prophecy and the truth of revelation.

"'He resolved to erect, without delay, on the commanding eminence of Moriah, a stately temple, . . . and to invite a numerous colony of Jews, whose stern fanaticism would be always prepared to second, and even to anticipate, the hostile measures of the pagan government.

"'Among the friends of the emperor . . . the first place was assigned, by Julian himself, to the virtuous and learned Alypius. . . . This minister . . . received an extraordinary commission to restore, in its pristine beauty, the temple of Jerusalem; and the diligence of Alypius required and obtained the strenuous support of the governor of Palestine.

"'At the call of their great deliverer, the Jews, from all the provinces of the empire, assembled on the holy mountain of their fathers; and their insolent triumph alarmed and exasperated the Christian inhabitants of Jerusalem. The desire of rebuilding the temple has in every age been the ruling passion of the children of Israel. . . . Every purse was opened in liberal contributions, every hand claimed a share in the pious labor, and the commands of a great monarch were executed by the enthusiasm of a whole people.

"'Yet, on this occasion, the joint efforts of power and enthusiasm were unsuccessful; and the ground of the Jewish temple, which is now covered by a Muhammadan mosque, still continued to exhibit the same edifying spectacle of ruin and desolation.

"'The Christians entertained a natural and pious expectation that, in this memorable contest, the honor of religion would be vindicated by some signal miracle.

"'"Whilst Alypius, assisted by the governor of the province, urged, with vigor and diligence, the execution of the work, horrible balls of fire breaking out near the foundations, with frequent and reiterated attacks, rendered the place, from time to time, inaccessible to the scorched and blasted workmen; and the victorious element continuing in this manner obstinately and resolutely bent, as it were, to drive them to a distance, the undertaking was abandoned."'

"Julian could have rebuilt a whole city with his wealth and power, but he could not rebuild a single temple. He began his work with a great flourish of trumpets, advertised to the whole world his purpose, and the reason for it: he was going to disprove the Bible prophecies and so destroy Christianity.

"Account for it as you please, two facts remain: First, Julian boasted he was going to disprove Bible prophecy by doing what the Bible said would not be done; second, with all the wealth and power of the world at his command, he failed."

Mr. Emerson stood up, and David Dare listened while he spoke. "Do you believe, Mr. Dare, that God predicted the event and then supernaturally intervened to see that His Word was not thwarted? Was it not rather the superstition of the workmen that defeated the project?"

"It is immaterial whether the workmen were discouraged by superstition or not. The prophets did not say how such attempts to rebuild were to be defeated. The public were invited by God Himself to defeat His prophecies if they could. Here was a man who boldly, boastingly accepted the challenge, put the power and wealth of the Roman Empire into the endeavor, and miserably failed. God had said all such attempts would fail. I am glad that if the endeavor was to be made, one who was wealthy, and who was more powerful than any man now living, tried it. No one else since Julian's day has made a similar experiment.

"Interesting as all this discussion has been to the student, the most important topic of all will be introduced next week: Christ—The Heart of Prophecy and History."

CHAPTER 10

CHRIST—THE HEART
OF PROPHECY AND HISTORY

Among the early arrivals were Mr. and Mrs. Emerson, accompanied by George and Lucile. But early as they were, others were already seated in the hall, discussing in earnest tones the points presented in previous lectures.

"There will be a big crowd tonight," ventured Lucile, as people came in increasing numbers.

"Naturally," replied her father. "From any point of view, this is the most important subject."

"Of the series?" she queried.

"No, my dear, the most important subject in all the world," he asserted, an unusual seriousness in his voice.

George and Lucile regarded their father in amazement.

"But—but, Dad," the girl finally stammered, "I thought you were an out-and-out unbeliever!"

"I am, but that does not prevent my realizing that no subject in all the world exceeds, or even approaches in consequence, the question of whether Jesus Christ lived, died, and rose again, as recorded in the New Testament."

Lucile still regarded her father with questioning and incredulous eyes.

"Do many infidels believe as you do about this, Dad?"

"Practically all. And the leading ones have so expressed themselves."

During this conversation George and Mrs. Emerson had been amazed and interested listeners. Soon the hall was filled to capacity, and still the crowds came. Mr. Dare was introduced by Dr. Morely.

"It is my intention," Mr. Dare said, "to consider only a very small part of the evidence bearing on the supremely important topic of today. Many valuable books, ably presenting the matter, merit your reading.

"All through His ministry Christ appealed to the prophets in proof of His startling statements. The appeal to prophecy was not only an argument to prove Jesus the Messiah, but frequently the sole argument. There are more than three hundred prophecies and references to Christ in the Old Testament that are expressly cited in the New Testament as predictions fulfilled in Him.

"And no one can say these predictions were written after Christ's time, for the last book of the Old Testament was written 400 years before Christ walked the streets of Bethlehem; or if we accept the extremely critical opinion, it was at least 168 years. So there could have been no collusion between the Old Testament prophets and the New Testament evangelists.

"On Christ's first public appearance He appealed to prophecy: 'This day is this scripture fulfilled in your ears' [Luke 4:21]. 'Then He said unto them, O fools, and slow of heart to believe all that the prophets have spoken' [Luke 24:25]. And to show His disciples how they should study the Bible, 'beginning at Moses and all the prophets, he expounded unto them in all the Scriptures the things concerning himself' [verse 27].

"However much skeptics may flout prophecy, they admit that the Old Testament does give frequent intimations of the coming of a remarkable personage. And they know that for ages the whole Jewish nation lived in eager expectation of a Messiah. And the surrounding nations, their enemies, knew that the Jews had this expectation, and mocked them because of it.

"Some of the passages upon which this expectation was founded were the promise of the seed of the woman in Genesis 3:15; the declaration that in the seed of Abraham should 'all the nations of the earth be blessed,' in Genesis 22:18; the statement that Shiloh was to come out of Judah before the dominion of that tribe should depart, as foretold in Genesis 49:10; that a prophet like Moses was to come, according to Deuteronomy 18:18, and quoted by Peter in Acts 3:22, as fulfilled in Christ.

"A remarkable part of prophecy foretold His inclusion of the Gentiles, whom the Jews hated. Yet they recorded and jealously preserved even that prediction. 'I will also give thee for a light to the Gentiles, that thou mayest be my salvation unto the end of the earth,' we are told in Isaiah 49:6. In Isaiah 60:3 the prophet says of God's people, 'The Gentiles shall come to thy light, and kings to the brightness of thy rising.'

"The prophecy about this coming Messiah was filled with startling paradoxes. In Isaiah 9:6 we are told that this Son of time is the Father of eternity; this weak Babe is the God of all might.

"The fifty-third chapter of Isaiah stated that the Coming One was to be cut off from the land of the living, a young man without offspring, yet He shall prolong His days, shall see His seed, which shall be so numerous that even He shall be satisfied.

He is to be put to death as a despised malefactor, to make His grave with the wicked, and yet the sepulcher of the rich is to be His tomb. He is to be scorned and rejected of men, and yet to justify many. He Himself is to be treated as a transgressor, and yet is to make intercession for transgressors. Perplexing paradoxes, these!

"So impossible did it seem that one person could fulfill the requirements, that many Jewish leaders said two persons were necessarily foretold. But now, since Christ has come, He fulfills every paradoxical requirement so naturally that we have ceased to observe the actual incongruity of the predictions. They no longer even seem incompatible.

"It is admitted that many centuries before the time of Christ, certain writings by Jewish writers foretold that a member of the Jewish nation, small and insignificant though it was, should be a blessing to all mankind. As we shall abundantly prove later, the most doubting scoffers proclaim enthusiastically that Christ has been and still is, above all others of the human race, a blessing— the greatest blessing—to all mankind.

"Account for it as you please, it is a stubborn fact that this obscure Jew of a small, despised, subject race has become most gloriously a blessing to every nation on earth. This strange prophecy that seemed to be born of the overweening egotism of a race has become a perennially amazing fact.

"Furthermore, the time of His coming was clearly marked. It was to be not only before the scepter departed from Judah, but while the second temple was standing. 'I will shake all nations, and the desire of all nations shall come: and . . . the glory of this latter house shall be greater than of the former, saith the Lord of hosts' [Haggai 2:7-9].

"But this is not all: Daniel gives the exact year of Christ's appearance as the Messiah, and of His crucifixion. [See Daniel 9:24-27 and Ezra 7:11-26 for the date of the decree, 457 B.C.] This is one of the best-established dates in all history.

"The 69 weeks, or 483 prophetic days, or literal years [see Num. 14:34 and Eze. 4:6], begin at 457 B.C. and reach to A.D. 27, at which time Christ was anointed as the Messiah by the Holy Spirit. [See John 1:29-36; Luke 3:21, 22; 4:18; Acts 4:27; 10:38; Mark 1:14, 15, marginal date.]

"The middle of the seventieth week, or seven-year period, brings us to the spring of A.D. 31, when the Messiah was to be 'cut off.'

"However one may attempt to explain it away, these prophecies and dates do fit exactly with the life of Christ, and nowhere else.

"From explicit passages in the writings of heathen historians Tacitus and Suetonius, we find a general expectation that an extraordinary person would arise in Judea about the time Jesus was born. So strong was this expectation among the Jews that many false messiahs appeared, appealed to the prophecies, and gained followers among those who were looking for the Messiah. So certain were the Jews that Jesus was not the Messiah, and that the temple could not be destroyed before the coming of the Messiah, that they refused all terms from Titus in A.D. 70, and fought with desperation to the last.

"To sum up: it is immaterial to me how you account for it, but several marvelously demonstrated facts stand out:

"1. Centuries before Christ was born a number of Jewish writers, living over a period of 1,000 years, boldly predicted that one of their race would be preeminently righteous.

"2. He would be a prophet.

"3. He would be rejected as the Messiah by the very people who foretold His coming, but would be accepted as the Messiah by every other nation on earth.

"4. He would be a blessing to all mankind.

"5. He would live in a certain definite, specified time.

"6. He would be killed.

"7. He would die as a malefactor.

"8. All these facts are testified to by prominent heathen writers.

"9. He was to be not merely a very superior human being, but God on earth.

"10. No one else meets these specifications, and Jesus Christ does.

"11. The truth of the system of Plato, or Karl Marx, or Buddha, or Muhammad does not depend on the question whether they were good or bad men. But if a flaw could be shown in the character of Christ, the whole Christian system would collapse utterly and at once.

"His character stands as the foundation of the whole Christian fabric. Skeptics know this, and still they do not attack, but uniformly praise Him! His character is so winning, so lovable, so beautiful, so strong, so perfect, that though, like Gilbert West, they begin their studies with the intention of attacking, they end in most enthusiastic praise, and often in worship.

"Christ runs through the Old Testament as well as the New, like the lifeblood through our bodies. He is the golden link that binds all its parts together, the light that illumes all its secret chambers, the key to its deepest mysteries and the keynote to its eternal harmony, the heart of every Bible book and prophecy."

Mr. Emerson, who had been quiet during the whole talk, arose to speak. David Dare turned in smiling expectancy to him.

"Mr. Dare," began Mr. Emerson in earnest tones, "I have refrained from interrupting you, for I have a real regard for the Christ, and do not want to appear in the role of a cheap disturber. But while your evidence regarding Him is interesting and not easily dissipated, it is far from convincing. For instance, Genesis 3:15, 'I will put enmity between thee and the woman,' etc., seems to me rather an unstable foundation on which to base a prophecy of Christ. And most of your other instances appear to me to be equally unsatisfactory."

"I agree with you, Mr. Emerson," replied Mr. Dare.

Lucile gasped, as did her brother and father and many others in the audience.

"You agree with me!" Mr. Emerson exclaimed. "I don't understand."

"Nevertheless, I agree with you. Any one of the more than three hundred predictions relating to Christ is insufficient to prove that He was the expected Messiah. But let me explain by relating an incident:

"The other day I was passing a rising skyscraper. A huge girder, weighing several tons, was being lifted high in the air by a cable, and riding the steel beam, in careless unconcern, was a man. Should the cable break, he would be dashed to certain death two hundred feet below.

"After the girder was placed, the cable, with the man riding the empty sling, was lowered again to take up another load.

While the next girder was being secured, I pointed to one of the small steel strands of which the cable was composed, and said to him:

"'Sir, don't you realize that not one of the scores of very small wires composing that cable would for a moment hold a hundredth of that load?'

"The laborer looked me over in contemptuous disdain. 'Say, fellow,' he laughed, 'don't you know that while one strand won't lift much, together they'll lift a girder ten times the weight of this here one; and don't you know that enough of these little strands woven together would lift a mountain?' He confidently stepped on the waiting load, gave a signal, and was swung aloft, as he mockingly waved me a farewell.

"The many prophetic strands taken singly will not prove much, but woven into a rope of evidence, they make a bond impossible to break. Other strands will be woven into our rope of evidence.

"In estimating the influence of Jesus on history," continued David Dare, "consider the difference between Christ and all moralists and philosophers. To gather all the wise and good precepts of all the different philosophers, and separate and discard all the error and gross immorality and absurd superstition in their teaching, would have been a great work. But that a single person, unacquainted with these philosophers, and unlearned in the wisdom of men, should, in direct opposition to the established practices and maxims of his own country, formulate a system so admittedly superior to all others challenges the studious attention of everyone."

Mr. Emerson arose. "Do you mean to imply that the philosophers were absurdly superstitious, and the moralists themselves immoral?"

"Exactly! That is just what I mean to say," said Mr. Dare. "No heathen moralist ever opposed himself to the prevailing vices and corruptions of his own time and country. No heathen moralist ever endeavored to curb the inhuman and horribly bloody sport of gladiators; none spoke against lust, the deliberate, slow killing of infants and slaves by exposure, or the public encouragement and establishment of brothels. The most amazing, indecent revelings were openly practiced as part of their heathen religion, and the greatest philosophers and moralists never lifted a voice against them."

Mr. Emerson interrupted again. "You surely cannot say these harsh things about such men as Plato, Socrates, Aristotle, and Seneca. These men at least were not guilty of the things you say."

The lecturer shook his head. "I am sorry to say that I must. Plato not only expressly allowed excessive drinking at the always-disgraceful festival of Bacchus—he and Aristotle both directed that means should be used to prevent weak children from being reared. Plato, Cicero, Epictetus, and other famous philosophers advised men to continue the idolatry of their ancestors. Diogenes and Socrates inculcated and practiced the most brutal lust, and Cato commended young men for frequenting brothels. Plato recommended a community of prostitutes, and advised that soldiers should not be restrained from even the most obscene and unnatural sensuality. And such things were encouraged and protected by the laws of the states. Solon, the great lawgiver, forbade lust only to the slaves. Zeno, the founder, and Cato, the ornament, of Stoic philosophy, and Seneca, the great moralist of Nero's time, were all suicides.

"In fact, the things that these men, the ornaments of ancient times, did and encouraged cannot possibly be related to a mixed audience, or to any audience."

"But they taught many fine things," insisted Mr. Emerson.

"Granted," replied Mr. Dare. "That is the point I am making. These men were admittedly the greatest of the heathen world, and the best they, who were the best, could give in life and precept was so poor that the human race was in a bad way indeed.

"But it is admitted by infidels, as I shall prove later, that Christ, with no secular education, so far outstripped all the moralists and philosophers combined that they rank a very poor second."

Mr. Emerson arose again. "You have presented very fair evidence that Christ fits the specifications of the predictions of the Old Testament. Even so, that does not prove that the religion of Christianity was established by Him."

"Well, let us inquire briefly into the establishment of Christianity," Mr. Dare replied. "That it exists and hence came into being in some manner, no one denies.

"There can be only two theories of its origin—it was founded either by impostors or by Christ.

"The propagation of this new religion was an exceedingly dangerous occupation from the first. To the Jews, Christianity was contrary not only to their long-established beliefs, but to those opinions on which were built their hopes and consolations.

"They looked for a Messiah to deliver them from the Romans. Even to think that these expectations might be disappointed enraged them. The whole doctrine of Christianity was novel and offensive to them. The extending of the kingdom of God to the Gentiles was a concept foreign to the Jews and certain to antagonize them, rather than win them to the new religion.

"Worse yet, it was necessary for the followers of Jesus to reproach the Jews with an unjust and cruel murder. This only made their work more difficult and dangerous. The disciples of Christianity had to contend with prejudice backed by power. They appealed to a people whom they first disappointed and then enraged—certainly a strange way of introducing a new religion.

"But this was only the beginning of difficulties. Christianity struck at the reigning power—at Rome—and made an enemy of every other religion in existence. It boldly denied at the very outset, and with no reserve, every article of heathen mythology and the existence of every god the heathen worshipped. It accepted no compromise. It could prevail only by the overthrow of every statue, altar, temple, and god connected with heathen religions.

"Christianity was not just another religion to be added to the one thousand already existing, but was a bold denouncing of all other gods as false, all other worship as vain and folly and deceit.

"Consider here another fact. The ancients regarded religion as entirely an affair of the state—not just allied to it, but an integral part of it. Thus an attempt to overthrow the religion of the state was regarded as a direct attack on the government, as treason punishable by death. And the early Christians knew this.

"Furthermore, the religious systems of the time had long been established. From ancient days their priesthood, endowments, rituals, and magnificent temples had witnessed to their power. Statuary, painting, architecture, and music contributed to their ornamentation, magnificence, and influence.

"These religions abounded in festivals to which the populace were devoted. Their religion, says Gibbon, 'was moreover interwoven with every circumstance of business or pleasure, of public or private life, with all the offices and amusements of society.'

"It is clear from the testimony of Pliny and Martial that the deaths of Christians were true martyrdoms; that is, they could have saved their lives at any time by joining the heathen exercises.

"And if Christ was put to death, could His followers expect to escape a like fate, especially in view of the fact that Christ told them death would be their fate? Even so, there was not the slightest tendency to draw back, even when confronted with the most terrible torture.

"These effects must be explained by adequate causes. When people in large numbers suffer horrible torture and certain death rather than merely continue in their former method of living in order to live, here is an effect that must have an adequate cause. And untold millions have thought Christ to be the adequate cause. Even infidels concede it, as will be shown.

"Furthermore, all accounts of the origin of Christianity agree. Both sacred and secular writers say the same thing: Christ was put to death in Jerusalem by authority of the Roman governor, Pontius Pilate. No contemporary or successor contradicts the story. Even the Jewish writers have not a word to the contrary.

"Neither Pliny in the first century, Celsus in the second, Porphyry in the third, nor Julian in the fourth, even suspected the authenticity of the New Testament or insinuated that the Christians were mistaken in the authors to whom they ascribed the New Testament.

"But here are the facts of a strange story that all these writers are agreed on: In the reign of Tiberius Caesar a number of people set about establishing a new religion in the world, and in the prosecution of this endeavor they voluntarily encountered great dangers, undertook great labors, sustained unheard-of sufferings, all for the story that a dead man, who was executed as a malefactor, had been raised to life. And this strange story has revolutionized history, changed the tide of empire, and altered millions of lives for the better.

"If the people who published this amazing story were not sincere, they were the biggest liars and fools ever on earth. They were villains for no purpose except to teach honesty, and with no prospect in life except to die a cruel death, execrated by all.

"Never in all the history of the world have men, women, and even children voluntarily undertaken lives of want, of incessant fatigue, of perpetual peril, submitting cheerfully to loss of home and country, to the endurance of stripes and stoning, to long and cruel imprisonments, and even to being torn asunder by lions or burned to death, for the sake of spreading abroad a story they knew to be false or that they thought might be false. People have never suffered these things for any other cause except for the Christian religion. People do not suffer all these things except for what they most earnestly believe. These facts are so well known that they are not denied by anyone, nor can they be explained away.

"Even skeptics of the most rabid type admit the beneficial effects of Christ's life as the most important influence ever to appear in the world."

Mr. Emerson stood once more. "You have made a number of references to what you are going to prove by unbelievers, but as yet have offered evidence from none of them. When may we have this proof?" His question was followed by an impatient murmur of assent.

"At the next lecture," replied David Dare. "And I will ask you, Mr. Emerson, to read these references from the books written by the skeptics, so that you may see for yourself and for the audience that the quotations are from the infidels I say, and are not misquoted. They will all be from the original books."

CHAPTER 11

Infidels Testify for Christ

After the Emersons were seated the next Sunday evening, Lucile leaned over to whisper: "Do you suppose, Dad, that he can really show that skeptics admit Christ to be the most important figure in all history?"

"I don't see how he can," replied her father, brows puckered in deep perplexity, "for if they do admit that, they will have to be Christians."

George, who had been listening, spoke up: "Probably he will quote only obscure writers."

Mr. Emerson considered this for a moment. "Sounds reasonable, George; I think you are right."

"I have noticed," observed Mrs. Emerson, "that Mr. Dare has so far always done what he has promised—yes, even more than you would expect from his words. I am confident he will produce leading, well-known skeptics to prove his point."

The other three members of her family regarded her in amazement. "Why, Mother," gasped Lucile, "has he converted you?"

"No, but I cannot help noticing that one by one the supposed unbreakable props supporting unbelief have been removed, until not many remain. It seems to me that the doubter's house is tottering. And now he promises to use unbelievers themselves to finish the work. I like the way he is doing this."

They looked in increasing surprise at the usually meek and quiet Mrs. Emerson. "But, Mother—" began George.

"Hush!" whispered Lucile. "Here comes Mr. Dare."

The speaker regarded his frankly impatient audience with a smile of welcome.

"I am glad to see you all back again. Last week we called attention to the fact that while we cannot now cross-examine the writers of the Gospels, they were cross-examined as no other witnesses have ever been examined since the world began.

"They were examined and cross-examined, not only by shrewd enemies like the Jews, astute reasoners like the Greeks, and nimble-minded lawyers like the Romans, but also by fire, sword, cross, flogging, and death. The Gospels are the only historical records in the world tested by the torture of the historians and of many who believed their accounts.

"Now, if we accept the writings of other historians whose veracity has not been tested by the scorching fire of persecution, how much more should we rely on the writings of the evangelists, whose accounts have been thus tested.

"The Man about whom the evangelists wrote would of necessity be amazingly unusual to inspire such unheard-of fidelity on the part of those who wrote about Him.

"But He was not only the most amazing, the most lovable, and the most powerful man in all history to the evangelists, but to modern skeptics as well—"

"Mr. Dare," interrupted Mr. Emerson, "you have made similar statements a number of times, but as yet have offered no evidence. With all due respect to your sincerity and truthfulness, we must have more than your say-so."

The ripple of applause drowned out the lecturer's first attempt to reply. The audience was clearly in a mood that demanded direct action.

"All right. You shall have it right now. Mr. Emerson, will you please come forward and read from these skeptical writers as I shall hand the books to you?"

"With pleasure," he replied as he made his way down the crowded aisle to the platform, where he was cordially greeted by both the lecturer and Dr. Morely, the chairman.

"I hand you this book," said the lecturer, holding out a large volume to Mr. Emerson. "Will you please tell this audience about the author and his writings?"

Mr. Emerson examined the volume in his hand, then spoke so all could hear:

"This is Volume II of *History of European Morals,* by William E. H. Lecky, who is also author of *History of the Rise and Influence of the Spirit of Rationalism in Europe.* Mr. Lecky was an Irish historian, statesman, and philosopher who died in 1903, and a leading unbeliever of his time and country. He wrote four large volumes to prove that rationalism is the only guide a reasonable man can follow."

"Then you would regard Lecky as a leading unbeliever of his day?" asked Mr. Dare.

"Decidedly," replied Mr. Emerson.

"Now please turn to pages 8 and 9 of the book you have, and read the passages marked," directed the lecturer.

Mr. Emerson's clear, strong voice was heard in every corner of the large auditorium as he read from the place indicated: "'It was reserved for Christianity to present to the world an ideal character, which through all the changes of eighteen centuries has inspired the hearts of men with an impassioned love; has shown itself capable of acting on all ages, nations, temperaments, and conditions; has been not only the highest pattern of virtue, but the strongest incentive to its practice; and has exercised so deep an influence that it may be truly said that the simple record of three short years of active life has done more to regenerate and to soften mankind than all the disquisitions of philosophers and all the exhortations of moralists.'"

"Thank you—that will do for the moment." Mr. Emerson seated himself next to Dr. Morely, while the lecturer turned to the audience, from whom subdued ejaculations of amazement were heard.

"Well, that was a center shot," gasped Lucile. Mrs. Emerson showed pleasure, and George looked puzzled.

"These words do affirm that Christ is the heart of all history; and not only that, but that three years of His life were more powerful for good than all the lives and productions of all the moralists and philosophers in the world. These are the words of a confirmed, avowed, world-renowned skeptic, written after years spent in carefully weighing all the evidence as an impartial historian.

"Such enthusiasm you might well expect to come from a warm believer, but I, equally with you, am amazed that such abounding extravagance of praise should come from a famous skeptic. But such is the fact, and it is not my business to explain it.

"If he were the only one to say such laudatory things, we might well regard it as a puzzling exception among the bold attackers of the Bible. But now I hand you another volume, Mr. Emerson. Will you please examine it and tell the audience about this writer?"

After a minute of examining the book, Mr. Emerson said: "This is *Nature, the Utility of Religion, and Theism,* by John Stuart Mill, an English economist and philosopher who died a few years before Lecky. He was likewise noted as a pronounced unbeliever."

"Very well," said David Dare. "Please read from pages 253-255, as indicated."

" 'Christ is still left; a unique figure, not more unlike all His precursors than all His followers, even those who had the direct benefit of His personal teaching. It is of no use to say that Christ as exhibited in the Gospels is not historical, and that we know not how much of what is admirable has been superadded by the tradition of His followers. . . . Who among His disciples, or among their proselytes, was capable of inventing the sayings ascribed to Jesus, or of imagining the life and character in the Gospels? Certainly not the fishermen of Galilee; as certainly not St. Paul, whose character and idiosyncrasies were of a totally different sort; still less the early Christian writers.

" 'When this preeminent genius is combined with the qualities of probably the greatest moral reformer, and martyr to that mission, who ever existed upon earth, religion cannot be said to have made a bad choice in pitching on this Man as the ideal representative and guide of humanity; nor, even now, would it be easy, even for an unbeliever, to find a better translation of the rule of virtue from the abstract into the concrete, than to endeavor so to live that Christ would approve our life.' "

"Observe," said the lecturer, "that Mr. Mill, the skeptic, specifically says that an unbeliever cannot do better than to live so that Christ would approve his life. That is perilously near to saying that skeptics should be Christians! I agree with him."

"But," interrupted Mr. Emerson, "Mill never did make the slightest profession of Christianity. I am puzzled by his words."

"I am puzzled, too; but there are his words, and when his skeptical friends remonstrated with him for writing them, he refused to have them omitted from successive editions of his book or to take them back. It is not for me to explain the inconsistencies of unbelievers, who say the most enthusiastic things about Christ and yet remain avowed unbelievers.

"All I am endeavoring to show is that the world's leading skeptics take occasion, after they have spent years fighting Christianity, to praise Christ and Christianity with the same verve and vigor one would expect of ardent Christians. And while these two are noted skeptics, they are not all who have sounded the praises of Christ and Christianity. I shall now call to the witness stand even more famous unbelievers than these."

David Dare handed a book to Mr. Emerson. "Please tell the audience who wrote this," said he.

Mr. Emerson examined the volume in question, turned to the crowd, and spoke so all could hear: "This is titled, *Journal of Researches,* and is written by Charles Darwin, the famous evolutionary naturalist."

"Would you class him as a Christian?" asked Mr. Dare.

"On the contrary, he cared nothing whatever for the Bible," responded Emerson. "He was noted as an unbeliever."

"During the years 1831 to 1836 Darwin circled the globe in the *Beagle,*" said the lecturer. "He reported that New Zealand was the darkest spot found on all his journey.

"After he returned to England, he found vigorous attacks being made against missionaries and missionary activity. Writing of those making these attacks, he made the statements Mr. Emerson will now read from pages 414, 425, 505.

Mr. Emerson turned to the pages indicated and read: " 'They forget, or will not remember, that human sacrifices and the power of an idolatrous priesthood—a system of profligacy unparalleled in another part of the world—infanticide, a consequent of that system—bloody wars, where conquerors spared neither women nor children—that all these have been abolished; and that dishonesty, intemperance, and licentiousness have been greatly reduced by Christianity. In a voyager to forget these things is base ingratitude; for should he chance to be at the point of shipwreck on some unknown coast, he will most devoutly pray that the lesson of the missionary may have reached thus far.'

" 'The lesson of the missionary is the enchanter's wand. The house has been built, the windows framed, the fields plowed, and even the trees grafted, by the New Zealander.'

" 'The march of improvement, consequent on the introduction of Christianity throughout the South Seas, probably stands by itself in the records of history.'

"Why did an avowed unbeliever write in defense of Christian missions after having expressed himself as sure they would utterly fail?" asked the lecturer after Mr. Emerson had handed the book back and seated himself. "Because he saw in person the indisputable evidence that his theory was wrong, and he had the honesty and manhood to confess his mistake. The results of the mission in New Zealand, which excited the surprise and elicited the eulogy of Darwin, are no different from the effects of Christian missions in every other part of the earth.

"Since skeptics generally will not concede the Bible to be more than a man-made book, why have they not given us a book to take its place? Since the majority of unbelievers think that the human race is constantly progressing—growing better—why don't they prove it by producing a better book? But they have not even attempted to do this!

"From the time of Celsus to the present, not a single rival has been put out by any skeptic or by any body of skeptics. There is no one book in all the world of which even one unbeliever, much less a thousand, will say: 'This is the wisest of books in all the earth; this is the book of books. Here all mankind may come for nurture of mind and elevation of heart and soul. Let's translate it into every language of earth, and go with it to every nation, kindred, tongue, and people, and, with sacrifice of life itself, show them a better way.' But skeptics do come very near to saying this of the Bible, as we have seen, and as we shall see further.

"Skeptics now have numberless printing presses and great schools, and they claim the greatest scholars. They have immense wealth, boundless leisure, all the advantages of science. The world has been ransacked from pole to pole, its highest mountains scaled, its deepest oceans sounded; its telegraph and radio have made immediately available the knowledge of all nations, and books have made the past accumulations of the whole world the servant of us all.

"The rocks beneath, the stars above, by use of microscope,

crucible, and telescope, have had many of their secrets wrested from them. Yet, with the advantage of all of this two thousand years' additional history and experience possessed by modern skeptics over the writers of the Bible, the skeptics have never even attempted to give us a book they claim to be better than the Bible. They usually spend the first twenty or more years after their maturity attacking the Bible, and, before ending their lives, devote a few thoughtful pages in refutation of their previous attacks and in enthusiastic praise of the very Book they had so long vigorously opposed.

"Thus it came about that Thomas Huxley, after writing many articles against the Bible, faced the issue and, realizing how important it was that something better be found, if possible, searched ancient and modern literature with eager eye for such a book. Not finding it, he pleaded for the use of the Bible in public schools as the source of highest education.

"Mr. Emerson," suggested Mr. Dare, "I am sure you can tell this audience what famous word was coined by Huxley."

"Yes," answered Mr. Emerson, "he coined the word 'agnostic,' meaning, 'one who does not know, an unbeliever.' He called himself an agnostic."

"I am handing you, Mr. Emerson, the Contemporary Review for December 1870, which contains an article by Huxley. Please read the passages marked."

All present listened carefully to these words: "'I have always been strongly in favor of secular education, in the sense of education without theology; but I must confess that I have been no less seriously perplexed to know by what practical measures the religious feeling, which is the essential basis of conduct, was to be kept up, in the present utterly chaotic state of opinion on these matters, without the use of the Bible. The pagan moralists lack life and color . . . . Take the Bible as a whole; make the severest deductions which fair criticism can dictate; . . . and there still remains a vast residuum of moral beauty and grandeur.

"'And then consider . . . that, for three centuries, this book has been woven into the life of all that is best and noblest in English history; . . . that it is written in the noblest and purest English, and abounds in exquisite beauties of a mere literary form; and finally, that it forbids the veriest hind who never left his village to be ignorant of the existence of other countries and other civilizations, and of a great past, stretching to the farthest limits of the oldest nations in the world.'"

"And now," said David Dare, "here is another word by Huxley, from a book entitled, *Science and Education*."

Mr. Emerson took the book and read clearly: "'By the study of what other book could children be so much humanized and made to feel that each figure in that vast historical procession fills, like themselves, but a momentary space in the interval between two eternities; and earns the blessings or the curses of all time, according to its effort to do good and hate evil?'[p. 398]."

He closed the book with a very sober expression on his face.

"Yes, this is the same man who spent several years in a heated debate with Gladstone over the Bible," said Mr. Dare. "Huxley later entered his protest against the 'heterodox Philistine' who found in the Bible 'nothing but a subject for scoffing and an occasion for the display of his conceited ignorance.' Then in another book, *Essays Upon Controverted Questions,* he makes it clear that his opinions as just exhibited to you were not momentary, but were a settled conviction." This book the lecturer also handed to Mr. Emerson. He read:

"'The Bible has been the Magna Charta of the poor and of the oppressed; down to modern times, no state has had a constitution in which the interests of the people are so largely taken into account, in which the duties, so much more than the privileges, of rulers are insisted upon, as that drawn up for Israel; nowhere is the fundamental truth that the welfare of the state, in the long run, depends on the uprightness of the citizen, so strongly laid down. . . . I do believe that the human race is not yet, possibly may never be, in a position to dispense with it [the Bible]' [pp. 39, 40]."

"Now, according to the great unbeliever Thomas Huxley, the best way to educate children, to inculcate morals, to aid the poor and oppressed, to instruct rulers and train citizens, is by means of the Bible," said the lecturer.

"We have found that leading unbelievers, one after another, have frankly turned to the Bible as the only source of moral and religious and practical education. In closing today's lecture I shall refer to another great scientist, a contemporary of Darwin and Huxley and nearly as well known, George Romanes. He was a pronounced skeptic. Shortly before his death he wrote some reflections on religion, born of his dissatisfaction with skepticism. He reviewed the whole field of moral and religious literature, hunting for the best, and at the close of his book, posthumously published, he sums up his convictions. I desire Mr. Emerson to read from *Thoughts on Religion*."

Mr. Emerson took the book, fingered it thoughtfully for a minute, and then read:

"'Not only is Christianity thus so immeasurably in advance of all other religions, it is no less so of every other system of thought that has ever been promulgated, in regard to all that is moral and spiritual. Whether it be true or false, it is certain that neither philosophy, science, nor poetry has ever produced results in thought, conduct, or beauty in any degree to be compared with it.' It is 'the greatest exhibition of the beautiful, the sublime, and of all else that appeals to our spiritual nature, which has ever been known upon our earth.' 'What has all the science or all the philosophy of the world done for the thought of mankind to be compared with the one doctrine, "God is love" ?' [pp. 170,171]."

Mr. Emerson stood as in a daze, looking at the words he had just read. A voice in the audience shouted, "Read that again." Others made the same request. So he repeated the passage, slowly, thoughtfully, almost reverently. As he finished and sat down, the whole audience was meditatively silent. Finally, David Dare spoke: "Had these glowing eulogies been written by some famous preacher, you might even then have expressed surprise at their warmth. But I must confess that I share your amazement that they are the expressions of world-famous infidels. Now, if the world leaders in unbelief issue such panegyrics on the Bible, Christianity, and Christ, why should any of you continue in unbelief? When the world's leading skeptics see in the Bible the most beneficent power on earth, it is high time we all gave it more careful study—"

Mr. Emerson arose to speak. "I have read these extracts with mingled emotions," he said. "I admit that I never imagined these men had said such things. However, influential as these men are known to have been, they are now dead, and have been dead from thirty to fifty years. Much has been discovered in the past thirty years to affect the beliefs of thinkers. I should like to know what leading living skeptics have said by way of admissions."

The applause that followed Mr. Emerson's words indicated a similar desire on the part of the audience. The lecturer stepped forward and said:

"Very well. Next week we will consider: Confessions of Leading Living Infidels."

CHAPTER 12

Confessions of Leading Living Infidels

The Emerson family arrived early. "Well," remarked George, looking around the already-crowded lecture hall, "the interest is as great as ever. And Dad seems worried."

Lucile nodded. "I'd be worried too, if I were in his place. He's the champion of what looks to be a losing cause. Here are more than eight hundred adults, at least half of whom are unbelievers, and all of them together can't answer the evidence produced by one man. Mr. Dare is slowly but surely backing them all into a corner."

"That's true," responded Mrs. Emerson. "First he produced an array of positive evidence in the nature of prophecies that no one here has been able to explain away. Then he showed by admissions of unbelievers themselves that they not only cannot deny the evidence showing Christ to be the greatest force ever to appear in this world, but they proclaim Him as ardently as any Christian. When the skeptics themselves concede nine tenths of the Christian's claim, what is left for which the skeptic can contend?"

Mr. Emerson regarded his wife in surprise. "So you think the skeptic's cause is lost?"

"Don't you?" she countered. He hesitated.

"Come now, Dad, 'fess up," teased Lucile.

"Is my whole family against me?" he smiled. "I'll answer you some other time, for Mr. Dare is beckoning for me to join him on the platform."

After a few words of greeting, the lecturer went straight into his subject. "I had planned to quote from many more noted unbelievers of recent times: Carlyle and Blatchford of England, Goethe and Strauss of Germany, Rousseau and Renan of France, and Tom Paine and Robert Ingersoll of America. All of these, though famous the world over for their agnosticism, have written words of ardent praise concerning Christ.

"But you ask for the opinions of living skeptics. You shall have them.

"Let us turn to that famous unbelieving radical, H. G. Wells. It is not necessary to identify him for this audience. Will you read, Mr. Emerson, the passages from his pen, marked in this July 1922 issue of the *American Magazine?*"

"With pleasure," replied Mr. Emerson, as he took the magazine:

" 'Jesus of Nazareth . . . is easily the dominant figure in history. I am speaking of Him, of course, as a man, for I conceive that the historian must treat Him as a man, just as the painter must paint Him as a man. . . . To assume that He never lived, that the accounts of His life are inventions, is more difficult and raises more problems in the path of the historian than to accept the essential elements of the Gospel stories as fact.

" 'Of course you and I live in countries where, to millions of men and women, Jesus is more than a man. But the historian must disregard that fact; he must adhere to the evidence which would pass unchallenged if his book were to be read in every nation under the sun.' "

"Notice the limits Wells sets for himself," interrupted the lecturer. "He speaks solely as a historian; he accepts only evidence that is unchallenged, and that would be accepted by every nation in the world; and yet observe the amazing conclusions he reaches. Will you please continue reading, Mr. Emerson?"

" 'Now, it is interesting and significant—isn't it?—that a historian, setting forth in that spirit, without any theological bias whatever, should find that he simply cannot portray the progress of humanity honestly without giving the foremost place to a penniless Teacher from Nazareth.

" 'The old Roman historians ignored Jesus entirely; they ignored the growth and spread of His teaching, regarding it as something apart from life. . . . He left no impress on the historical records of His time. Yet, more than nineteen hundred years later, a historian like myself, who does not even call himself a Christian, finds the picture centering irresistibly around the life and character of this simple, lovable Man.

" 'We sense the magnetism that induced men who had seen

Him only once to leave their business and follow Him. He filled them with love and courage. Weak and ailing people were heartened by His presence. He spoke with a knowledge and authority that baffled the wise and subtle.

" 'So the historian, disregarding the theological significance of His life, writes the name of Jesus of Nazareth at the top of the world's greatest characters.' "

"How different are these statements from those one would expect avowed unbelievers to make," said David Dare, as Mr. Emerson returned the magazine and sat down. "They are forced by the stern facts to pay such astounding homage to Christ and Christianity. If even half of what the skeptics say of Christ and Christianity is true, it is clear that there is nothing else, no other influence in the whole wide world, that is worthy to be named in the same breath.

"I could quote in detail from the writings of unbelievers themselves how Christianity has freed the slave, stopped infanticide as a common public practice, established hospitals, raised the position of women, brought liberty, and changed the lives of millions for the better. All these things we may infer from the statements of H. G. Wells. Now, Mr. Emerson, who would you say has taken the place of Ingersoll in America as a leading doubter?"

Mr. Emerson considered a minute. "Well, H. L. Mencken, editor of *American Mercury* and author of a number of very modernly rationalistic, sophisticated books, not only fills his place, I would say, but has made a definite place of his own. He is certainly much better educated than Ingersoll, as sneering as Voltaire, and as modern as Bernard Shaw."

"I have here a book of Mencken's published in 1930, called *Treatise on the Gods.* I have marked a number of passages for you to read, if you will," said David Dare.

Mr. Emerson opened the book to page 227 and read:

" 'The historicity of Jesus is no longer questioned seriously by anyone, whether Christian or unbeliever. The main facts about Him seem to be beyond dispute.'

"Now turn to page 255," directed the lecturer.

" 'It is not easy to account for His singular and stupendous success. How did it come about that One who, in His life, had only the bitter cup of contumely to drink, should lift it Himself, in death, to such vast esteem and circumstance, such incomparable and world-shaking power and renown?'"

"Now, according to Mencken," said Dare, "Jesus has power to shake the earth, and he admits frankly that he cannot account for His having this power. But that is not all. Please read pages 266 and 267."

"'Unless the whole New Testament is to be rejected as moonshine, it seems to be certain that many persons saw Him after His supposed death on the cross, including not a few who were violently disinclined to believe in His resurrection. Upon that theory . . . the most civilized section of the human race has erected a structure of ideas and practices so vast in scope and so powerful in effect that the whole range of history showeth nothing parallel.'"

"Mencken has a violent dislike for the Jews, and expresses it vigorously," the lecturer went on to say. "I mention this because I do not agree with him, and also to show that he makes his own case more difficult by this attitude. The mystery of how the Jews could produce such literature as the Bible amazes us no less than it amazes Mencken. Now read pages 345, 346, and 347, please."

"'The Bible is unquestionably the most beautiful book in the world.'"

"Just a minute, Mr. Emerson," interrupted Mr. Dare. "To hear skeptics talk on the street corner and to hear them arguing with ministers, you would think the Bible the most revolting book in the world. But here is America's most noted living agnostic telling us that without any question the Bible is the most beautiful book in the world. This is an admission that skeptics can show nothing to compare with. But read on."

"'Allow everything you please, . . . no other literature, old or new, can offer a match for it.

"'Nearly all of it comes from the Jews, and their making of it constitutes one of the most astounding phenomena in human history. For there is little in their character, as the modern world knows them, to suggest a talent for noble thinking. . . . The Jews could be put down very plausibly as the most unpleasant race ever heard of. As commonly encountered, they lack many of the qualities that mark the civilized man: courage, dignity, incorruptibility, ease, confidence. They have vanity without pride, . . . and learning without wisdom. . . .

'Yet these same Jews, from time immemorial, have been the chief dreamers of the race, and, beyond all comparison, its greatest poets. It was Jews who wrote the magnificent poems called the Psalms, the Song of Solomon, the books of Job and Ruth; it was Jews who set platitudes to deathless music in Proverbs; and it was Jews who gave us the beatitudes, the sermon on the mount, the incomparable ballad of the Christ Child, and the twelfth chapter of Romans.

" 'I incline to believe that the scene recounted in John 8:3-11 is the most poignant drama ever written in the world, as the Song of Solomon is unquestionably the most moving love song, and the twenty-third psalm the greatest of hymns.

" 'All these transcendent riches Christianity inherits from a tribe of sedentary Bedouins, so obscure and unimportant that secular history scarcely knows them. No heritage of modern man is richer and none has made a more brilliant mark upon human thought, not even the legacy of the Greeks.

" 'The story of Jesus . . . is touching beyond compare. It is indeed the most lovely story . . . ever devised. . . . Beside it the best that you will find in sacred literature of Muslim and Brahman, Parsee and Buddhist, seems flat, stale, and unprofitable.' "

As Mr. Emerson returned the book and sat down, the lecturer stepped to the edge of the platform and spoke:

"There is much more from these agnostic writers, Wells and Mencken, that I would like to quote. But these extracts serve to show that these ultramodern skeptics admit that Jesus is historical, that the Gospels are in the main true, that Jesus is the most powerful force in all the world. You have heard Mr. Emerson read these statements from their own productions."

"But," interrupted Mr. Emerson, "why is it that while it is true unbelievers make such statements, they still do not become Christians? If they put any great store by the views you have had me read, why haven't they ceased their skepticism and become Christians?"

Murmured applause followed his questions. David Dare

turned smiling to Mr. Emerson, then back to the audience:

"A very good question, and perfectly proper and logical. It is not my place to say why Wells, Mencken, Lecky, Mill, and others whom I quoted have still, in the face of these admissions, called themselves skeptics. But it is a fact that a large number who were unbelievers have left their skepticism and become ardent, professing believers. Next week it will be our privilege to consider some of them."

CHAPTER 13

CONVERTED SKEPTICS

The Emerson family had comfortably seated themselves and greeted a few friends, but still it was not quite time for the lecture to begin.

"I can't help admiring the workmanlike way in which David Dare has gone about his task," observed Lucile. "Instead of simply saying that many prophecies cannot be denied or explained away by unbelievers, he produces them and invites the unbeliever to do his worst. And, frankly, so far the unbeliever hasn't done very much."

"That's a fact," agreed her brother. "And instead of saying skeptics admit Christ to be the greatest character of all time, he has Dad on the platform reading it out of the skeptics' very own books. I call that a clever move. I wonder who the converted infidels he promised to tell us about tonight are."

"You may be sure," said Mrs. Emerson, "that they are more than ordinary unbelievers."

"I agree with you all," said Mr. Emerson, smiling. "Mr. Dare is handling this whole discussion in a most original and pleasing manner. He has indulged in no cheap sarcasm, has given every speaker a fair, courteous hearing, and has answered all questions in a clear, convincing manner. And—but there he goes to the platform."

The lecturer nodded to several with whom he had become acquainted, among them the Emersons, and began:

"Two infidels once sat in a railway car discussing Christ's wonderful life. One of them said, 'I think an interesting romance could be written about Christ.'

"The other replied, 'You are right; and you are just the man to write it. Set forth the correct view of His life and character. Tear down the prevailing sentiment as to His divinity, and paint Him as He was—a mere man among men.'

"The suggestion was acted on, and years later the romance

appeared. The man who made the suggestion was Colonel Robert Ingersoll, the world-famous infidel; the author was General Lew Wallace; and the book was *Ben-Hur*.

"In studying his sources—the Gospels—for material to write the romance, General Wallace found himself facing the unaccountable Man Jesus. The more he studied Christ's life and character, the more profoundly he was convinced that He was more than a man among men.

"He was amazed by the fact that out of an obscure Galilean village, so mean and low that its very name was a reproach, came this young man, versed in neither Greek nor Hebrew—a young carpenter who had hardly been outside His province, but whose first public utterance, the Sermon on the Mount, is the most original and revolutionary address on practical morals the world has ever heard.

"Lew Wallace, like the rest of the world, wondered at His words. Age has not dimmed their light, lessened their appealing sweetness, or diminished their force. Familiarity has not spoiled their freshness or destroyed their fragrance. His words shine out peerless as ever, the sweetest, calmest, wisest words ever spoken to men.

"Lew Wallace discovered Christ to be the person that literature feels to be its loftiest ideal, philosophy its highest personality, criticism its supreme problem, theology its fundamental doctrine, religion its cardinal necessity, and every man his closest friend.

"He found Christ to be the great central fact in the world's history. To Him everything looks forward or backward; all lines of history converge in Him and radiate from Him. At last, unable to resist the evidence, Lew Wallace, the infidel friend of the infidel Ingersoll, was constrained to cry, like the centurion under the cross, 'Truly this was the Son of God.' So in the writing of *Ben-Hur,* a book that was to exhibit Christ merely as a very human man, Lew Wallace was converted, and painted Him as the Son of God.

"About ten years ago Europe was thunderstruck by a book about Christ. The author had been noted as a most rabid atheist. He says that he 'affronted Christ as few men before him have ever done.' He wrote sneering books, letting his 'mad and voluble humor run wild along all the roads of paradox' and 'negation' to arrive at 'perfect atheism.'

"He went on to say that he did not turn to Christ 'out of weariness, because his return to Christ made life become more difficult and responsibilities heavier to bear; not through the fears of old age, for he could still call himself a young man [he was forty]; and not through desire for worldly fame, because as things go nowadays he would receive more commendation if he continued in his old ideas.' In short, after one has written books attacking Christ and Christianity, and is noted as a leader of infidels, it is indeed hard to turn around and confess he has been mistaken.

"But this is what Giovanni Papini, the renowned and self-proclaimed atheist, did. His *Life of Christ* so amazed the world that it has been translated into all the leading modern languages. I read it with tingling delight."

Mr. Emerson stood, and obtained recognition. "I have not interrupted, because I desired to hear your stories of 'converted infidels' fairly complete. But these men never left their own countries to investigate. They merely read the Bible, a few histories, and changed their minds. While it is evidence that unbelievers do become believers—which we knew before—it is hardly convincing."

"You admit that Lew Wallace, Papini, and others changed their views after reading the Bible and a few histories," replied Dare. "Well, few skeptics bother to make that much research, and not one in a thousand ever reads the evidence on both sides. But I will now tell you about an unbeliever who electrified the doubting as well as the Christian world by announcing that he was going to demonstrate that the Bible could not be true.

"Sir William Mitchell Ramsay, in 1881, was a young man of sterling integrity, unimpeachable character, culture, and high education. He had a sincere desire to know the truth. He had been educated in an atmosphere of doubt, which early brought him to the conviction that the Bible was fraudulent.

"He had spent years deliberately preparing himself for the announced task of heading an exploration expedition into Asia Minor and Palestine, the home of the Bible, where he would 'dig up the evidence' that the Book was the product of ambitious monks, and not the book from heaven it claimed to be. He regarded the weakest spot in the whole New Testament to be the story of Paul's travels. These had never been thoroughly investigated by one on the spot. So he announced his plan to take the book of Acts as a guide, and, by trying to make the same journeys Paul made over the same routes that Paul followed, thus prove that the apostle could never have made them as described.

"The enemies of the Bible were enthusiastic over what they were confident would prove a complete and final refutation of the Book; and it must be admitted that some believers trembled at the prospect. For this was the boldest attempt to disprove the Bible since the days that Julian, the emperor of Rome in the fourth century, set himself with his army and wealth to annihilate belief in the Bible by deliberately breaking its prophecies—a project that miserably failed, as Gibbon, the infidel historian, admits.

"The factor that made the Ramsay expedition unique was the confidence that its leader inspired from opposing camps. Here was a man who was not a boisterous blasphemer, content to sit in Paris, London, or Berlin, and from these remote points assail a book that had its origin and setting in ancient Palestine. He had the courage of his convictions and the intellectual and physical equipment to carry out his purpose to make investigation. So all parties believed in Ramsay, and when he said he would publish his findings just as he discovered things to be, his word was accepted.

"Equipped as no other man had been, he went to the home of the Bible. Here he spent fifteen years literally 'digging for the evidence.' Then in 1896 he published a large volume entitled *St. Paul the Traveler and the Roman Citizen*.

"The book caused a furor of dismay among the skeptics of the world. Its attitude was utterly unexpected, because it was contrary to the announced intention of the author years before. The chagrin and confusion of Bible opponents was complete. But their chagrin and confusion increased, as for twenty years more, book after book from the same author came from the press, each filled with additional evidence of the exact, minute truthfulness of the whole New Testament as tested by the spade on the spot. The evidence was so overwhelming that many infidels announced their repudiation of their former unbelief and accepted Christianity. And these books have stood the test of time, not one having been refuted, nor have I found even any attempt to refute them.

"Quotations cannot do justice to forty years' exploration and writing, but I cannot refrain from a few extracts. Speaking of the book of Acts, Ramsay, on page 238 of his *St. Paul,* says:

" 'The narrative never makes a false step amid all the many details, as the scene changes from city to city.' And on page 240: 'Every minute fact stated in Acts has its own significance.'

" 'The characterization of Paul in Acts,' says Ramsay on pages 21 and 22, 'is so detailed and individualized as to prove the author's personal acquaintance. Moreover, the Paul of Acts is the Paul that appears to us in his own letters, in his ways and his thoughts, in his educated tone of polished courtesy, in his quick and vehement temper, in the extraordinary versatility and adaptability which made him at home in every society, moving at ease in all surroundings, and everywhere the center of interest, whether he is the Socratic dialectician in the agora of Athens, or the rhetorician in its university, or conversing with kings and proconsuls, or advising in the council on shipboard, or cheering a broken-spirited crew to make one more effort for life. Wherever Paul is, no one present has eyes for any but him.'

"Turn now to one of his later books, *The Bearing of Recent Discovery on the Trustworthiness of the New Testament,* published in 1914. In the introduction, page v, he says: 'My aim . . . is to show through the examination, word by word and phrase by phrase, of a few passages which have been exposed to hostile criticism, that the New Testament is unique in the compactness, the lucidity, the pregnancy, and the vivid truthfulness of its expression. That it is not the character of one or two only of the books that compose the New Testament: it belongs in different ways to all alike.'

" 'From Strauss to Schmiedel, what a series of distinguished and famous scholars have blindly assumed that their inability to estimate evidence correctly was the final and sure criterion of truth'[p. 254].

" 'Such progress as the present writer has been enabled to make in discovery is largely due to the early appreciation of the fact that Luke is a safe guide' [p. 259]. 'Wherever the present writer followed Luke's authority absolutely, . . . he was right down to the last detail' [p. 262].

"And so it happened that Sir William Ramsay, who set out to destroy belief in the Bible, has done more than any other one man in modern times to establish, to demonstrate beyond possibility of cavil, the absolute, minute trustworthiness and truth of the New Testament.

"Also I would like to tell you of Adolf Deissmann, the great young German scholar whose findings rank second only to Ramsay's. He began his investigations in similar mood to Ramsay's. After years of exploration he arrived, as had Ramsay, at a setteled belief in the very Bible he had expected to disprove. Deissmann's *Light From the Ancient East* is the most revolutionary book on the Bible of this century as Ramsay's was of last century. Together, these two men, who set out as doubters determined to explore and prove for themselves the unreliability of the Bible, have erected an indestructible Gibraltar of evidence in its favor. Until the evidence of these two men has been overcome, the cause of unbelief is lost.

"This subject has only been touched; and now I must close. But I commend to you the thrill of joy you will certainly experience if you follow these men in their fascinating adventures of exploration in Bible lands and truths.

"Next week we will consider what the skeptic has to offer us."

CHAPTER 14

What Has the Skeptic to Offer?

As the Emerson family waited for the crowd to gather, Mr. Emerson looked frankly worried. Lucile leaned past her brother George and daintily passed her hand across her father's brow.

"Why the deep furrows of thought, Dad? They'll mar your style of beauty," she said teasingly.

"I am worried," he admitted.

"What about?"

"I'm unsettled, entirely at sea. I was certain my favorite objections would be unanswerable. But Mr. Dare has answered most of them, and has presented a number of insuperable arguments for Christianity."

"Why haven't you had your skeptical friends help you?" asked George.

"I have put Mr. Dare's arguments to them, and they are unable to reply. No one here has been able to answer them. And now he is going to come right into our citadel and attack our defenses. And I know that we are almost defenseless. Our strength is in attack."

"Then why not attack?" asked Lucile, eyes alight with hope for a contest.

"Because I have already brought forward my best arguments, and they have been answered. To bring forward weaker ones would be evidence of weakness and an anticlimax. I am not interested in trivialities. I am not interested in quibbling about where Cain got his wife, how Balaam's ass could talk Hebrew, how iron could float, how Jonah could live in a whale three days, how the sun stood still, or any of the other stock sneers, which after all amount to little when placed alongside the tremendous fact of Jesus Christ and His life here on earth and His wonderful words."

"Why, Dad!" exclaimed Lucile and George in openmouthed astonishment. "What has happened?"

"I don't know yet," he smiled.

"I do," said Mrs. Emerson, also smiling. They turned to her for explanation, but checked their questions when they saw the lecturer mounting the platform.

"It is with reluctance that I approach this subject," said David Dare. "I do not relish attacking the beliefs of another; I should much rather present the affirmative side of Christianity. But I really see no escape from considering what the unbeliever offers us when he endeavors to destroy Christianity. Since he sets himself up as having something superior to Christianity or he would not try to destroy it—we must carefully examine what he proposes in its place and weigh it thoughtfully."

Mr. Emerson arose, and turning to the audience spoke:

"I know we are all pleased with this very courteous attitude of the speaker, and I for one assure him that he need have no hesitation in speaking his mind."

Hearty applause followed Mr. Emerson's words.

"Thank you," smiled the lecturer in recognition of this expression of friendliness. "You all know that Robert Ingersoll, the renowned skeptic, had a brother whom he dearly loved. Standing by the side of his brother's grave, Robert preached the funeral sermon, uttering in the course of his remarks what has been admired all over the world, by his brother skeptics, as the acme of his genius.

"In the face of the majesty of death, in the presence of the unknown, the veil of the skeptic's mind was torn aside, his suffering soul laid bare, and there were wrung from his blanched lips these famous words that have circled the earth:

"'Whether in mid-sea or among the breakers of the farther shore, a wreck must mark at last the end of each and all. And every life, no matter if its every hour is rich with love and every moment jeweled with joy, will, at its close, become a tragedy, as sad, and deep, and dark as can be woven of the warp and woof of mystery and death. . . . Life is a narrow vale between the cold and barren peaks of two eternities. We strive in vain to look beyond the heights. We cry aloud, and the only answer is the echo of our wailing cry.'

"To me, sadder words were never uttered. Life, to Ingersoll, after he had plumbed its depths and scaled its heights, was only a cold and barren tragedy, its highest aspirations but a hideous mockery. He faced 'the blackness of darkness forever,' as Jude 13 has it.

"Whatever else skepticism is, it is not and cannot be the truth. It does not even profess to be a truth. It is admittedly only a negation, a putting out of the candles of others without lighting any in their place, an attempt to plunge the world into the darkness that infidels admit exists in their minds.

"Let us now turn to another great unbeliever, Herbert Spencer. After having written some score of volumes, in all of which he either attacked or ignored Christianity, he sat down at the close of a long life to write his autobiography in two large volumes. Near the end of the second volume he talks of death, and writes with evident horror of his own end. He goes on to lament the fact that in death 'there lapses both the consciousness of existence and the consciousness of having existed.' In other words, one cannot be 'consciously dead,' as Lecky puts it in his *Map of Life*.

"In fact, Herbert Spencer so yearned for rest for his soul that immediately following his words about death he goes on to say: 'Thus religious creeds, which in one way or the other occupy the sphere that rational interpretation seeks to occupy and fails, and fails the more it seeks, I have come to regard with a sympathy based on community of need, feeling that dissent from them results from inability to accept the solutions offered, joined with the wish that solutions could be found.' [*Autobiography,* Vol. II, p. 549].

"A number of important conclusions follow:

"First, Spencer knew his own solutions had failed, that they were not solutions. He says so. For fifty years he had used his giant mind in an endeavor to solve the riddles of existence apart from the Bible. At the end of his life he admits how utterly futile have been his efforts.

"Second, the more skepticism tried to occupy the field of religion and account for existence apart from religion, the more it failed.

"Third, he so keenly realized his need of a solution that he abandoned his own and all other skeptical explanations, and sought for solutions in Christianity. Though he did not accept the Christian solution, he admitted it is the best offered.

"Fourth, his own active antagonism changed at last to a sympathy with Christianity before his death, and he actually voiced a wish that he might be a Christian. If his words do not mean all of this, then words have no meaning.

"Now, why should we discard the Christianity which he regarded with such sympathy and desire, and embrace what he threw away?

"But let us come to the present. In the *American Magazine* for November 1930, beginning on page 23, is an article by a noted writer W. O. Saunders. Let us listen to him:

"'I would have you meet one of the lonesomest and most unhappy individuals on earth.... I am talking about the man who doesn't believe in God.... I am not asking you to meet the man who denies there is a God—the atheist; I am asking you to meet that wistful, pathetic, and lonely fellow who simply says he does not know—the agnostic, the man who has no God. Some call him an infidel.

"'I am peculiarly qualified to introduce the agnostic. I am an agnostic myself. Out of my own life, my own heart, and my own mind I write this. In introducing myself, you will have an introduction to the agnostic in your own neighborhood, for he is everywhere in the land.

"'Probably you will be surprised to know that the agnostic envies you your faith in God, your settled belief in a heaven after death, and your blessed assurance that you will meet with your loved ones in an afterlife in which there will be neither sorrow nor pain. He would give anything to be able to embrace that faith and be comforted by it.

"'For him there is only the grave and the persistence of matter. All he can see beyond the grave is the disintegration of the protoplasm and psychoplasm of which his body and its personality are composed.

"'But in this material view I find no ecstasy nor happiness. Is this the end and all of human life and endeavor? ...Therefore would I try to convey to your mind and heart something of the wistfulness and loneliness of the man who does not believe in God.

"'Your agnostic may put on a brave front and face life with heroic smiles. But he is not happy.... Standing in awe and reverence before the vastness and majesty of the universe, knowing not whence he came nor why, appalled by the stupendousness of space and the infinitude of time, humiliated by the infinite smallness of himself, cognizant of his frailty, his weakness and brevity, think you not that he, too, sometimes yearns for a staff on which to lean? He too carries a cross.

"'Your agnostic … is … tremendously impressed by the power of your faith. He has seen drunkards and libertines and moral degenerates transfigured by it. He has seen the sick, the aged, and the friendless comforted and sustained by it. And he is impressed by your wonderful charities, your asylums, your hospitals, your nurseries, your schools.… He must shamefacedly admit that agnostics, as such, have built few hospitals and few homes for orphans.

"'To him this earth is but a tricky raft adrift upon the unfathomable waters of eternity, with no horizon in sight. His heart aches for every precious life on the raft, drifting, drifting, drifting, whither no one for a certainty knows.…

"'You have met one of the lonesomest and most unhappy individuals on earth.'

"What, then, has the infidel to offer? Nothing; nothing at all. He says so. He is wistfully envious of the Christian. He is lonesome and unhappy. Then what has he to offer the Christian? Nothing but his own unhappiness and lonesomeness."

"But, Mr. Dare," interrupted Mr. Emerson, "the agnostic cannot accept Christianity, because so much has to be taken on faith, contrary to what he sees as natural law. He cannot order his life by faith; he must govern himself according to facts. The reason the agnostic has nothing to offer is that he knows nothing about the afterlife, and to act on faith alone is absurd."

"On the contrary," smiled Mr. Dare, "that is exactly what you do, and what every other human being does."

"I don't understand," said Mr. Emerson, in a puzzled tone. "I wish you would explain."

"Gladly. All mankind, educated and ignorant, artists and scientists, idealists and materialists, believe in things they have never seen and cannot prove. Mathematicians believe in axioms; chemists, in atoms, cosmic ether, and contradictory attributes in bodies; astronomers, in the incomprehensible infinity of space;

natural scientists, in invisible natural forces and natural laws. For our own peace of mind we lay down the law that bodies have eternally attracted each other and that they will eternally do so; but we know nothing about it and can prove nothing of the kind.

"According to the great scientist Thomas Huxley, even science is largely a matter of faith. In his book *Evolution and Ethics* he says: 'If there is anything in the world I do firmly believe in, it is the universal validity of the law of causation; but that universality cannot be proved by any amount of experience' [p. 121]. And then in his *Science and Christian Tradition* he says further: 'The ground of every one of our actions, and the validity of all our reasonings, rest upon the great act of faith' [p. 243].

"The knowledge of infidels is only faith resting on dogmas concerning existence, the forces of nature, matter, atoms, mechanics. Everyone, Christian and infidel alike, lives by faith.

"It is amusing to find that the very man who derides miracles believes in the self-creation of the world; to hear the man who mocks at the creation of the world by God speak learnedly of unconscious matter producing consciousness, of a primal cell that created itself! He denies the soul of man, but maintains the soul of atoms and believes in the unconscious memory of molecules! He maintains the self-beginning of life, and denies the possibility of creation!

"The skeptic has nothing but a wail of despair and a sob of loneliness to offer the groping seeker for help. The infidel finds it easier to spend his time criticizing the Bible and Christians than in providing aid for helpless humanity. But the very skeptics who smile at our faith, admit that they live by faith. The very skeptics who tell us we are foolish to believe in Christ admit they envy us our belief in Him. The very skeptics who so vigorously advise us to give up our Christianity admit they have nothing whatever to take its place, and would give anything if they could have the comfort and happiness such a belief gives.

"So next week, in our last lecture, we will consider what Christianity has to offer."

CHAPTER 15

WHAT CHRISTIANITY HAS TO OFFER; CONVERSION OF THE EMERSONS

The crowd gathered early for the last meeting of the series. The buzz of conversation indicated the intense interest. Small groups in different parts of the hall were engaged in lively discussion.

Lucile's eyes were bright with excitement. "I wonder if anything is going to happen," she remarked to her father.

"A great deal is going to happen, my dear, but not what you seem to expect. There will be no controversy tonight."

"Why not, and what will happen?"

"There will be no controversy, because all important points of controversy have been covered, and the subject tonight is too vital to all of us for thoughtless interruptions."

"But what will happen?" she persisted.

"I cannot be sure," Mr. Emerson smiled as he observed her earnestness, "but I expect decisions to be made that will affect the whole life of many present."

Lucile turned to face her father squarely, while George and Mrs. Emerson watched in breathless interest. A new seriousness was in Lucile's voice as she asked:

"Have you made your decision, Dad?"

"Not yet, but I expect to do so. I want to hear first what Christianity has to offer. Have you decided?" He put the question to his daughter.

"Yes, I have, Dad. I hope you don't object."

"You know I don't. And you, George?" George merely nodded his head solemnly in the affirmative. "And you, wife?" Mrs. Emerson, with an appealing look in her soft brown eyes, answered quietly, firmly:

"Yes; I have always felt a yearning to be a Christian."

Suddenly the hall was quiet, for the speaker and the chairman were going to the platform. David Dare, as he arose to speak, was received by a subdued but apparently unanimous applause.

"What has Christianity to offer you?" he began. "You have heard the very frank admissions of leading skeptics that skepticism has literally nothing whatever except blank despair and soul-terrifying loneliness for the unbeliever. You have listened to the wistful yearnings uttered by these skeptics.

"You have seen how the Bible foretells, even down to the end of time, the history of all the leading nations of the ancient world. Not one of you present, nor anyone else, for that matter, has been able to deny that these prophecies were made centuries before their fulfillment; and no one can account for them on natural grounds. It is admitted by all of you that no other book in the world contains real prophecies. The prophecies of the Bible present an unexplainable mystery to the unbeliever.

"Christianity has Christ to offer you. This, according to the testimony of nearly a score of leading infidels, whose words were read here, is the greatest fact in the history of the world. They waxed more enthusiastic over Him than over anyone else in the world. And finally some leading unbelievers publicly renounced their unbelief and admitted joyously their belief in Christ.

"Let us consider for a bit what Christ means to the human race, and therefore to you personally. As the direct result of Jesus' story of the good Samaritan, and His other teachings of mercy, and His own personal tender care for the sick, the horrible practice of exposure and neglect of the sick and maimed is now, and has long been, a thing of the past. Care of the sick or injured in hospitals and sanitariums—humane treatment of disease—is now the rule wherever the Bible has gone.

"Are you a social reformer and interested in the poor? Then consider how the poor have been uplifted by Him. Slavery has been abolished by the teaching of Jesus that all men are of one blood, and brothers in the sight of God. Jesus offers comfort to the oppressed and boldly arraigns the selfish rich. He calls not for the palliatives of charity, but for fundamental social justice for all.

"Do you believe that education is a fundamental in the progress of humanity? Then observe that knowledge has been promoted by Him. Jesus sought to make men whole in mind as well as in body. When Jesus said, 'Go ye therefore, and teach all nations'

[Matt. 28:19], He released, He impelled, the greatest forces directed into the world. There are almost infinite implications in that command. It directs all Christians to scan the history of nations, so as to apply the gospel to every phase or relationship of life.

"To this end, methods of navigation had to be studied and perfected in order to reach all nations, as commanded. This command has unloosed untold energies of men in every age, sending them into the depths of the earth and upon wings above the clouds; to the burning sands of the Sahara, to the chill and solitudes of the Arctic, and to the great unknown fastnesses of Tibet. Why? That the Great Commission may be carried out.

"The command to teach all nations means that the teacher must know more than the learner. So under the missionary urge of Jesus' words, more than nine hundred languages have been reduced to writing, and all kinds of practical as well as religious books have been translated into them by the missionary. In fact, the geographical knowledge of our globe has come largely from the missionaries who have ventured where the foot of the trader dared not tread.

"The race from which Jesus came was the most hated and the most persecuted in the world, and was at the same time the most bigoted and provincial. Yet He became the one universal Man, uniting Orient and Occident, appealing equally to the East and to the West.

"Socrates taught for forty years, Plato for fifty, Aristotle for forty, and Jesus for only three; yet those three years infinitely transcend in influence the combined one hundred thirty years that Socrates, Plato, and Aristotle, the three greatest men of all antiquity, taught.

"Jesus was not a writer, yet He is quoted more than any writer in history, and His words have winged their way to earth's remotest bounds, and have been translated into all languages and nearly all dialects.

"So far as we know, the Carpenter of Nazareth drew no architectural plans, yet the world's masterpieces of architecture have been reared in His praise.

"He painted no pictures, yet the paintings of Raphael, Michelangelo, and Leonardo da Vinci received their inspiration from Him.

"He wrote no poetry, but Dante, Milton, and scores of the world's greatest poets were inspired by Him.

"He composed no music, still Haydn, Handel, Beethoven, Bach, and Mendelssohn reached their highest perfection of melody in the hymns, symphonies, and oratorios written in His praise.

"Jesus was highly social, yet He possessed a reserve that discouraged all familiarity. His temperance never led to bigotry or austerity. He was not conformed to the world, yet He was attentive to the needs and sufferings of all men.

"Skeptics praise the clearness of His judgments, the depth of His ethics, the justness of His decisions, the weight of His words, the faultless beauty of His glorious life—its balance, its pure nobility, and its serene power.

"You never exhaust Christ's words. They pass into proverbs, they are enacted into laws, they are consolidated into doctrines, they become consolation for the poor and weary, they grow into the life and transform the character; but they never pass away, and after all the use made of them, they are still as fresh as when first spoken.

"Christ's words have the charm of antiquity with the freshness of today, the simplicity of a child with the wisdom of God, the softness of kisses from the lips of love, and the force of lightning rending mountains.

"The most determined criticism has not been able to dethrone Christ as the incarnation of perfect holiness. The waves of a tossing and restless sea of unbelief break at His feet, but still He stands the supreme model, the inspiration of great deeds, the rest for the weary, the fragrance of all the world, the one divine flower in the garden of the world.

"Skeptics quite freely admit these things, and attempt to account for Christ on natural grounds. They are very willing to admit Him to be the greatest man that ever lived, but at any hint of actual deity in combination with His humanity, they arise in determined protest and violent rejection of such a suggestion.

"However, by calling Christ a superman they have by no means solved the difficulty. On the contrary, they have created more difficulties than they had before. For if Christ is not in a real sense God as well as man, He must be the world's greatest deceiver, for He claimed that worship was due Him, that He was the light of the world, that He preexisted, that He descended from heaven, that He was equal with God [John 5:17, 18], 'that all men should honor the Son, even as they honor the Father' [John 5:23; see also John 10:30, 38]. Jesus accepted the title of 'the Lord thy God' [Matt. 4:7; John 10:33]. When Thomas the skeptic, after Jesus' resurrection, called Him 'my Lord and my God,' Jesus did not rebuke him, but on the contrary said unto him, 'Because thou hast seen me, thou hast believed: blessed are they that have not seen, and yet have believed' [John 20:28, 29]. There is much more written, all to the same effect, in all four Gospels.

"To have made the claims He made, if none of them were true, would necessarily brand Him as the most unprincipled deceiver in all history. Yet there is not a skeptic who will admit He was anything of the kind. You all, equally with me, believe that Christ was honest and earnest, for you know that a bad man could not have taught such great truths as He taught, and that a good man could not have deceived the people for whom He gave His life.

"Thus at once the greatest difficulty in the Bible and the weightiest proof of its inspiration is Christ. He stands out commandingly among all the sons of men, unapproached and unapproachable. He walks down the ages with the tread of a conqueror, while around Him shines a moral splendor that has compelled even the most hostile criticism to bow the head in hushed reverence. Upon the impregnable Rock of Ages all criticisms are baffled and shattered. Christ is, as He prophesied He would be, the great spiritual magnet that draws all men everywhere to Himself.

"From heaven, with the accumulated love of eternity in His heart, came this King of kings, to be one with humanity, to suffer the vilest mockery, to endure the strongest temptations. and to experience the lowest of deaths, that you and I might know what love is, and be restored to Edenic innocence and happiness. Around Him all truth clusters and revolves, as do the planets about the sun.

"And now will you pardon me a personal testimony?

"I was reared an infidel. My parents and other immediate relatives were proud of their unbelief. I was nourished on the vaunting skeptics of the ages.

"But I observed the futile amazement with which every skeptic from Celsus to Wells stood around the cradle of the Christ. I wondered why this helpless Babe was thrust into the world at a time when Roman greed, Jewish hate, and Greek subtlety would combine to crush Him. And yet this most powerful, devastating combination ever known in history served only to advance the cause of the Infant who was born in a stable—the purest human being in the world born in the filthiest place in the world.

"I marveled that this poverty-stricken, uneducated plebeian, who exercised no authority, commanded no army, held no office, received no honors, wrote no books, and who died in early manhood the most contemptible of deaths, a malefactor on a cross between two criminal—I marveled that His name is yet the most esteemed name on earth, even among the skeptics themselves.

"No unbeliever could tell me why His words are as charged with power today as they were nineteen hundred years ago. Nor could scoffers explain how those pierced hands pulled human monsters with gnarled souls out of a hell of iniquity, and overnight transformed them into steadfast, glorious heroes who died in torturing flames, that others might know the love and mighty power of the Christ who had given peace to their souls.

"No agnostic could make clear why seemingly immortal empires pass into oblivion, while the glory and power of the murdered Galilean are gathering beauty and momentum with every attack and every age.

"Nor could any scoffer explain, as Jesus Himself so daringly foretold, why by telephone, airplane, and radio, by rail, horse, and foot, His words are piercing the densest forest, scaling the highest mountains, crossing the deepest seas and the widest deserts, making converts in every nation, kindred, tongue, and people on earth.

"No doubter could tell me how this isolated Jew could utter words at once so simple that a child could understand them and so deep that the greatest thinkers cannot plumb their shining depths. The life, the words, the character of this strange Man are the enigma of history. Any naturalistic explanation makes Him a more puzzling paradox, a fathomless mystery.

"But I learned that the paradox was plain and the mystery solved when I accepted Him for what He claimed to be—the

Son of God, come from heaven a Savior of men, but above all, my own Savior. I learned to thrill at the angel's words: 'Behold, . . . unto you is born this day . . . a Savior, which is Christ the Lord.' Now I have learned the great truth that " 'though Christ a thousand times in Bethlehem be born, if He's not born in thee, thy soul is still forlorn.'

"This, then, is what Christianity has to offer: a perfect Model, forgiveness of sins, rest to the soul, a Comforter, a Companion, a Savior, and then eternal life in communion with myriads of perfect beings. Contrast this with the bewailing despair, the glum hopelessness, the wearing heartache that is ever the lot of the unbeliever. Which will you choose? The choice is yours, the opportunity now. You have had weeks to weigh the evidence, to feel the thrill of joy in contemplating the Christ. He asks to enter your heart and bring His peace that follows His forgiveness of sins."

Then pausing a moment, his earnest eyes searching the faces of that solemn audience, he said:

"Those who desire to abandon their unbelief and publicly proclaim their acceptance of Jesus as the divine Son of God, their Savior from sin; those who were formerly skeptics and who desire to be known henceforth as Christians, followers of the Christ, please stand."

More than a hundred rose instantly to their feet. David Dare's eyes turned instinctively to the section where the Emerson family usually sat. His face lighted with pleasure when he saw all four of the Emersons standing.

"Mr. Emerson," he said, "I am happy to see you and your family give this testimony. Will it embarrass you to tell the audience briefly why you have taken this stand?"

"I shall be only too glad to do so." Mr. Emerson's voice was clear, and thrilled with joy as he spoke. "While you have been carrying on these lectures, I have been reading the Bible through. Many things I thought the Bible said, I found it did not teach at all, and many cavils I thought objections, I found vanished before a candid study. Then when I read the New Testament, I found in Jesus peace and contentment for the first time in my life. The terrifying feeling that I was alone in a vast universe, left to grope my way in an infinitude, gave way to one of perfect trust when I grasped the hand of Jesus, the One who created all these things.

"The knowledge that my wrongs, my mistakes, my sins, no matter what they are, have been forgiven is the most wonderful thrill in all the world. The dread with which I looked forward to my remaining years has turned to a fountain of joy and praise to the Jesus for whom I have always had a high regard, but whom I now trust in as my own Friend and Savior."

David Dare then asked all who were standing to come forward to meet him, and make arrangements for uniting with the church, so that they might have a part in the organized work of giving to all the world "this gospel of the kingdom." Among the first to reach him were Mr. Emerson; Mrs. Emerson, in quiet content; George, in whose soul had been born a new ambition to serve; and Lucile, the once pert, thoughtless girl, now chastened with a new beauty of soul.